THE SCIENCE-BACKED
MANIFESTATION BREA

MANIFEST
LIKE YOU
MEAN IT

THE MANIFESTATION
REVOLUTION

BIANKA VÁRNAI

Manifest Like You Mean It

Start With Purpose

Startwithpurpose.online

Disclaimer Page

Dedication

This book is for **you.** For the one who felt something profound inside, something real, something powerful, but never quite knew how to bring it to life. For the one who tried, fell, got back up, and still wondered if they were meant for something more.

If you have felt stuck, unseen, or unsure if their dreams are too big, unrealistic, or just not meant to happen. I know that feeling too well. I've been there.

Waking up with a vision in your heart, but you see no clear path to make it real. You feel stranded on one side of a canyon, but the life you truly want is on the other. Just too far to reach. I feel you!

Your dream isn't random; it's there for a reason. It has a purpose.

And maybe this book is the very moment that changes everything. So, let yourself believe in endless possibilities, because something greater out there has a plan for you that you can't let go.

You have the power to create the life you want, and it has been inside you all along. And now, it's time to discover it.

With all my belief in you,

Bianka Várnai | Start With Purpose

Sneak Peek – Before You Read Another Page...

I am in the car with my father, handling an errand.

It's just a regular day... until I realized it isn't.

Within 2 minutes, something mind-blowing happens.

Two completely unrelated **synchronicities** appear, seemingly uninvited.

It feels like the **universe is whispering to me** directly through objects, timing, and words.

And all I could think is:

What is happening?

Is this a coincidence?

Or something **much bigger?**

• • •

Another Synchronicity:

...Something rare is showing up in his life...twice.

Through wildly different channels, through an emotionally charged moment. A country. An object. A brand. Each one improbable.

It's **jaw-dropping!**

His world is transforming.

He feels like **life has responded to his energy.**

These events aren't just spiritual.

They're neurological.

It's energy.

It's real!

• • •

Your Reticular Activating System—**RAS**—is your brain's filter.

It processes **11 million bits** of data every second, but only lets through **0.001%** of your perceived reality.

That's unbelievable!

You only see what your subconscious believes matters.

So what happens when that filter gets **hijacked** by repetition, emotion, and rhythm?

• • •

You've tried the affirmations. Pinned the vision board. Whispered your desires with love and light. But it **left you in the dark**, only hoping someone would hear. But nothing changed.

Why?

Because your brain didn't believe it. Your body didn't feel it. Your world just couldn't respond.

It's science.

• • •

This isn't about hope. It's about rewiring.

Through a revolutionary method, called **Impact Rap.**

It's not just a practice.

It's a performance of your future.

And your subconscious is the **audience.**

Rhythm, emotion, and movement are designed to get past your conscious mind and **rewrite the script** underneath.

You don't just say yes to the universe.

You scream a full-body **YES.**

What you're about to discover isn't theory.

It's manifestation revolution!

Introduction

This book is your frequency shift. You've landed here for a reason. This isn't wishful thinking.

If you're holding this book, it means you are ready for profound transformation! You are done waiting. Done repeating affirmations that never really worked. Done watching others manifest breakthroughs while you feel stuck in limbo. Because no matter how much you've journaled, visualized, or meditated... **something was always missing.**

And that missing piece wasn't just a technique. It's how your energy shows up. Your body. Your rhythm. Manifestation isn't about what you want. It's about who you believe you are in the moment.

The truth is, we've been introduced to a watered-down version of manifestation. One that sounds comforting but doesn't match how your brain and your energy actually work.

It left you thinking you needed to be more patient. More positive. More "high vibe" and results will follow. But you don't need more time. You don't need more effort. You need to start activating your brain so effectively, that **your dream life comes rushing through your front door.**

This Revolution Starts With You

This is a movement!

It's the wake-up call for every part of you that's been hoping to move forward and experience positive change, but didn't know how to get there.

If you've been watching life happen instead of creating it, let this moment be the beginning of a new era. **The era when you win.**

Stepping in with your whole body, showing up with your potent energy and activated nervous system.

This book will show you how to become your own powerhouse and **"generate your own gravity,"** so that **life** comes to you.

You'll learn why the Reticular Activating System (RAS) determines whether you see opportunities or miss them. Why affirmations fail without rhythm, repetition, and emotional charge, and why speaking your dreams is not enough.

This is Manifest Like You Mean It! And it starts with YOU.

Today

Table Of Contents

The Manifestation Myths That Keep You Stuck

• • •

"The greatest enemy of knowledge is not ignorance; it is the illusion of knowledge."

— Stephen Hawking

Before we start, we need to clear something up.

You've been steered off course.

Not out of malice but out of simplification. You've been presented with a watered-down, feel-good, quote-style manifestation that just doesn't have the depth to work. You've been told to stay high vibe, think happy thoughts, and wait for the universe to deliver. Like you're ordering your dream life through an online store. That's not how it works. And deep down... you know that.

So before we dive into rewiring your brain and bringing your future into your present, we need to burn some myths to the ground. Because if we don't, they'll keep whispering in the background, sabotaging everything you're about to build. **Let's call them out one by one.**

Are you ready?

Myth #1: You Have to Be Positive All the Time

This is one of the most toxic lines in manifestation culture. That you'll mess up your manifestation if you feel sad, angry, tired, or frustrated (just human). Like one bad mood will cancel your efforts.

But the truth is...suppression isn't alignment. Real power comes from feeling everything fully, without getting stuck in the process. Fundamental transformation requires your free-flowing energy.

Some of the most potent manifestations I've ever seen were born out of joy, frustration, and even sadness.

Although these are very different emotions, they have two things in common: **clarity and action.**

So, you don't always need to *"be high vibe."* You need to be real, feel your emotions, and learn how to move your energy with intention. That's what Impact Rap helps you do.

Stop chasing constant positivity. That's not alignment, it's denial dressed as light. Real alignment is raw, honest, and alive. Cry if you need to. Just **don't stop moving.**

Myth #2: You Just Have to Believe

Nope. Sorry. If belief was enough, we'd all be millionaires with perfect lives by now.

Belief is a starting point, but not a magic spell.

You can believe in your dreams and still live the same life every day. If your subconscious identity still screams, *"This isn't me,"* nothing changes.

I mean, nothing! And definitely not your actions and habits.

Belief must be backed by embodiment. By action, movement, emotion, energy. That's what turns belief into reality. That's what builds your life, atom by atom.

Have you heard the story of a man who desperately wanted to win the lottery and kept praying to god for help to win? Then one day God replied. *"Please, please... just buy a lottery ticket."*

So you can see, belief opens the door to possibilites, but action is what walks you through it. You can't manifest by waiting. **Buy the ticket!**

Myth #3: If It's Not Easy, It's Not Meant for You

Let me say this: Ease doesn't always mean alignment.

Growth will push you, the transformation will challenge you, and sometimes your manifestations come with **discomfort,** detours, and full-on tower moments. That is normal.

It's the learning curve that your evolution requires.

Your dream life won't always feel "safe and comfortable." It will feel expansive. Don't confuse the two.

Ease can mean alignment but so can **resistance**. The key isn't how it feels. It's whether it's growing you.

The universe doesn't just hand over your dream life; it invites you to rise to it. Not through **suffering,** but through discomfort. If the path demands more truth, more integrity, or more **action,** that's alignment in motion.

Because most of the time, what's testing you isn't here to stop you. It's here to **evolve you.**

Myth #4: You Just Have to "Let the Universe Do Its Thing"

Look, co-creation means **co-creation,** not passive hoping. You are not just a receiver. You're a **creator.** You get to shape your reality, move, speak, act, and decide.

The universe supports you. It will show you synchronicities. But you can't just wait and watch. You need to "do. " You need to ignite the magic through your own clarity and actions. That's what this whole book is about.

So now it's time for you to take action. You're not blocked. You're not broken. You've just been taught myths that stole your superpower.

But now **we take it back.**

This isn't just myths-busting. The "good vibes "police just got fired. The "just believe" propaganda was destroyed. That whole "wait for the universe to do it for you "? We canceled it. This is a rescue mission for your dreams. You don't need to fake-smile anymore. You don't need to chant empty mantras you don't fully believe. **You need neural activation! You need real fire. Emotions. Action.** This is the part where you **Manifest Like You Mean It.**

So fasten your seatbelt, and let's build something real!

CHAPTER 1

The Truth About Manifestation Why It Works, Why It Fails, and How to Fix It

• • •

"What you think, you become. What you feel, you attract. What you imagine, you create."

— Buddha

Before we unpack all about manifestation, let's clean our *"imaginary windshields "*and have an honest look at our starting point.

I know you have tried everything, but deep down, you felt that something was always off. It felt forced. **You are not the problem.**

It's time to be honest with ourselves: Flat, emotionless affirmations won't change your life. A vision board you made once and never looked at again won't rewire your brain. Wishing and hoping won't bring you closer to your goals.

You gave it all you got, and it didn't bring results. I know you are tired, and maybe even lost all hope. But don't worry, this isn't where your story ends.

In this book, you'll learn how to make manifestation work for you backed by science. **No fluff.**

Just action and results.

Now, le"'s unpack what manifestation is and why it's not what you think.

What Manifestation Really Is (and Why It's Not What You Think)

Manifestation isn't magic. It's not about waiting for your dreams to be delivered by some cosmic delivery man. Manifestation is **training your brain** to see, act, and create in alignment with your vision. The part of your brain called the **Reticular Activating System (RAS)** is in charge of that. It sits right at the base of your brainstem. A powerful filter that determines what you notice, ignore, and when you perceive opportunities.

Have you ever bought a new car and then, out of nowhere, started seeing that exact model everywhere? It's not like everyone suddenly went out and bought the exact vehicle overnight. **Those cars were always there;** you just weren't noticing them before. That's your **(RAS)** at work. Your brain filters reality every second of your life, working behind the scenes. So most of the world around you, you don't even notice.

Right now, your brain is being hit with **millions** of tiny details: every sound, movement, scent, and piece of light hitting your eyes. If you had to process all of it at once, you'd be completely overwhelmed. If your mind processed everything equally, you'd be paralyzed by sensory overload. Your RAS acts like a **bouncer** at an exclusive club, deciding what gets in and what gets ignored. Deciding only to let in the thoughts, ideas, and external influences that match what you tell it is important.

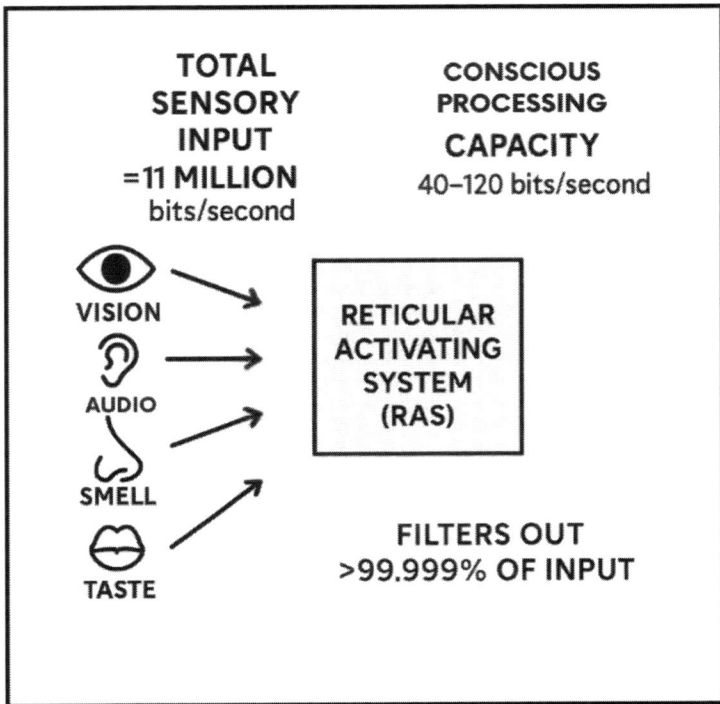

TOTAL SENSORY INPUT
=11 MILLION bits/second

CONSCIOUS PROCESSING CAPACITY
40–120 bits/second

VISION
AUDIO
SMELL
TASTE

RETICULAR ACTIVATING SYSTEM (RAS)

FILTERS OUT >99.999% OF INPUT

So it filters over 11 million bits of information per second yet only allows 40 to 50 bits into your conscious awareness. That means **99.99%** of reality is ignored. And that's powerful!

That's why, when you think of something you really like or want, you suddenly start seeing that exact thing **everywhere.** Your brain wasn't paying attention before because it wasn't programmed to do so. The same thing happens with everything in life.

What you focus on, what you really, deeply pay attention to, your brain starts pulling into your view. It **highlights what "matters "and blocks out the rest.** The moment something becomes important to you, your brain starts letting it through into the "important" bucket. You see connections you would have missed previously. You recognize chances and opportunities you wouldn't have noticed or acted on before. And that's when things begin to shift.

What you focus on intensely and repeatedly becomes what your brain starts **filtering for.** And that's exactly why manifestation works when you do it right. And here's the wildest part: You can **train your brain to your advantage.**

But what ultimately signals to your RAS what's important? **Repetition, focus, and emotional intensity.**

So imagine what happens when you constantly tell yourself, I'm not good enough, *I'm always broke, and nothing ever works for me.* Unfortunately, we tend to believe negative things about ourselves much more easily, and repeat them much more often than anything we would like to manifest.

So your RAS will actively filter the world around you to reinforce that belief. It will **blind you to opportunities** because your brain doesn't think they matter. You won't notice the job offer that could change your career. You won't take the chance to introduce yourself to someone who could transform your life.

But what happens if you calibrate your RAS with intense visualization, emotion-packed statements, and repeated words that feel real?

It will start to filter the world to show you the path toward those experiences, goals, and visions. **Your brain will start treating your vision as reality.** It will begin working to close the gap between you and the things you desire. It will start **"speeding up time,"** so you experience whatever your RAS is filtering for quicker.

Why Traditional Manifestation Fails (and How to Stop Wasting Time)

What do you think is the most significant reason manifestation doesn't work for most people? **They lack emotional charge.** Because the truth is that manifestation can only be as powerful as the **emotional intensity** behind it. **Let's have a closer look:**

Flat Affirmations Lack Emotional Charge: Most people repeat affirmations like *I am wealthy. I am successful.* But deep down, they don't believe it. Their voice is weak, and there's no emotional connection. So basically, it feels like a joke, and your brain knows that too. It won't respond to empty words, but to real emotions. **Impact Rap** injects energy, rhythm, and conviction into your affirmations, making **your subconscious listen.**

Vision Boards Without Emotion Inducing Pictures and Action: Cutting out pictures and sticking them on a board won't change your life, unless it **triggers** genuine beliefs, intense emotional responses and deeply moves you from within. But repetition is also essential. A vision board without **active engagement** is just decoration. So, if you plan on glancing at it once a month, don't even bother making one.

Journaling is powerful for self-reflection, but it can lack urgency. Writing down your dreams is helpful, but it doesn't activate your body's energy systems the way speaking, moving, and engaging with rhythm does.

Manifestation Without Embodiment: If you say one thing but live another, your brain gets mixed signals. You can't just visualize success and expect your life to turn around; you have to **act and feel in alignment with your desires.**

So, you can see that there can be many reasons why manifestation attempts have failed in the past. But there is something very important to clarify before we can manifest anything. And yes, it's the classic **"what do I actually want"** question. Because how are we going to get anything if we don't know what it is?

Sometimes, we can feel unsure about what we want in life, about what we truly desire. Life can get very confusing, and we can lose touch with where we are even headed.

You're not alone. Many people struggle with figuring out their direction and lack **clarity** about what truly fulfills them deep inside.

Don't worry! This book will help you take action while you gain clarity along the way.

But if you want to dig much deeper and understand your inner mechanisms; not only what you desire the most but also your innate strengths and the hidden truth of what would give you the most meaning and joy in your life, then I have good news! **I'm working on something for you.**

The Purpose Equation-Find the Missing Pieces, Shatter Stagnation, and Step Into the Life You Were Born to Lead

This book is your blueprint to unearth your authentic life path from beneath all the conditioning, aimlessness, and stagnation. It delivers a radical formula to unlock your **purpose ecosystem**, packed with real-life stories of finding purpose and a no-nonsense guide to living your truth. It will show you a clear path lit by your potential.

Don't just wait for purpose to find you! Scan the **QR code** and be the first to grab *The Purpose Equation!

Don't miss out! This is your chance to see behind the curtain, discover why you're here, and unleash your ultimate potential. So flip the script, and win **BIG** this time! Join **The Movement and Live with Purpose!**

But let's get back to the book! Now, we'll explore a concept that will blow your mind and allow you to manifest like a pro! I bet you're ready. **Let's go!**

Manifestation that Works

To manifest what you want, you need a method that:

- **Activates your emotions fully** (so your brain believes it's real).

- **Engages your body & energy** (so it's not just mental, it's physical).

- **Moves you to take action** (because no action = no results).

That is exactly why traditional methods don't cut it. And this is where **Impact Rap** gets in the picture. A powerful method that will change everything that was going wrong before and will turn your manifestation experience into a **radical breakthrough** instead of another failed attempt with no results.

But for now, I have a question for you.

I can't help but wonder... **is manifestation even real?** I've seen things happen that made me stop in my tracks. Not just once. Over and over again. And I want you to know about them. They made me seriously question what is going on. Get ready! **This will blow your mind!**

The Phone Number and the Washing Machine

I was talking on the phone with a friend. We had some catching up to do. As we started talking, he warned me that it wouldn't be an average story. Then he began to speak. I was all ears!

He explained that his mother had a used washing machine for which he created an online advertisement months ago, but it hasn't been sold. **Nobody called** the phone number attached to it.

After that, he discussed some issues they needed to resolve, which turned into a confrontation. As he remembered this moment in detail, it was apparent that he was experiencing **heightened emotions** at the time, and not the happy ones. He was frustrated and angry, but was able to pinpoint something very peculiar.

During that confrontation, he couldn't stop thinking about money, and one thought occupied his mind: "I **need to get money fast.**"

Right after that conversation, still buzzing with intensity, they decided to switch the phone number on the washing machine ad. Instead of his, they put the number of the person renting the apartment where it was stored. It just seemed more convenient. It's no big deal. But this is where it got interesting.

Within 30 minutes, two phone calls come in. **Two serious buyers.** One of them **bought the washing machine** that same day. Let me repeat that: No ad renewal. No extra visibility. No changes to the listing, just a new phone number. After months of nothing... suddenly, **it's sold in half an hour.**

It's mind-blowing! I was so stunned by his story!

He couldn't believe it had been sold in 30 minutes, while nobody had called for months. He kept asking, **"How did this even happen?** What changed?"

The ad was buried. The machine was the same. Nothing else shifted... as it seemed so. **So what really happened?** What made this possible? And what made it so quick? Let's break it down!

We start with stagnation and non-action. The washing machine isn't being sold, and no one calls the phone number. Then something happens.

A conversation, a **confrontation**. Thoughts about money and the need for it. Feelings of **frustration** and slight anger.

Then, there is an **action.** The phone number attached to the advert is being changed. And something in there made all the difference in the universe.

Was it **speaking** about both finances and the washing machine in one conversation that made this possible? Was it action, heightened **emotions**, or thoughts of money, that made all the difference? Or were they needed altogether for a change that we perceive as a positive one?

Now, let's look at my personal experience, which might **reveal more about this mystery.**

The Keychain and the Submersible

I was in the car with my father, just handling an errand. It was a regular day. I was going to my storage room to collect a piece of furniture I had sold, so I asked my father to be a helping hand. My intention was to get rid of things I didn't need anymore and create more financial safety, as I was about to adopt a sweet shelter dog.

I realized I didn't have the right **keys** for the place, as the locks had recently been changed. I had to ask the company for a new key. So there we went. We were in a rush, so when we arrived, I grabbed the key and didn't even look.

Now, we were back on track. Later in the car, I noticed something dangling on the key chain...something unusual. I looked closer, and you **will not believe** what I saw!

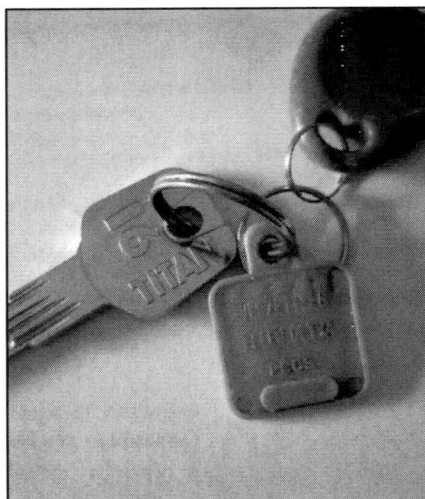

To my biggest surprise, there was a retro plastic tag from the 90s that said, "Vaccinated Against Rabies" in hungarian. I gasped! My eyes widened. This is wild! -I said **What are the odds?**

But my father was not so impressed and just kept on talking about some news he heard, something about a tourist submarine accident. Right after that, for some reason I looked down to my hands and saw something else.

Engraved into the key was the word **TITAN.** As I'm sure you have heard, the sad news that a submersible exploring the wreckage of Titanic had an accident that claimed lives; it was called **TITAN.**

Now, that had an effect on my father as well. We were both completely shocked at how this **double synchronicity** just happened. I could not wrap my mind around it. Was it my gentle, **unconditional love** toward that sweet shelter dog I would save, that drove this to occur? Was it the conversation, the **spoken words,** that made this possible?

Well, something did.

It was apparent that something is happening, but I couldn't explain what exactly it is. My curiosity was sparked for life! **How on earth is this possible?**

In pursuit of finding the key to these mysteries, I began to ask everyone I knew, hoping that someone else had a similar story to mine. And **sure, they did.**

So now, I would like to tell you their stories.

This is an acquaintance's experience in a beautiful place with her friends.

The Cows by the Water

She told me about an incident that happened to her during a holiday. She was near a small town on a riverside with her friends. They sat in the sand, talking away and admiring the breathtaking views. She was mentioning something to them; a story about some cows.

Note: As I write this, I decided to boost my brain with sugar and I grabbed the first sweet thing laying around on the table. You wouldn't be able to guess what my choice of sweets was. It's a caramel, packaged in the old-fashioned way. Guess what was on the packaging!

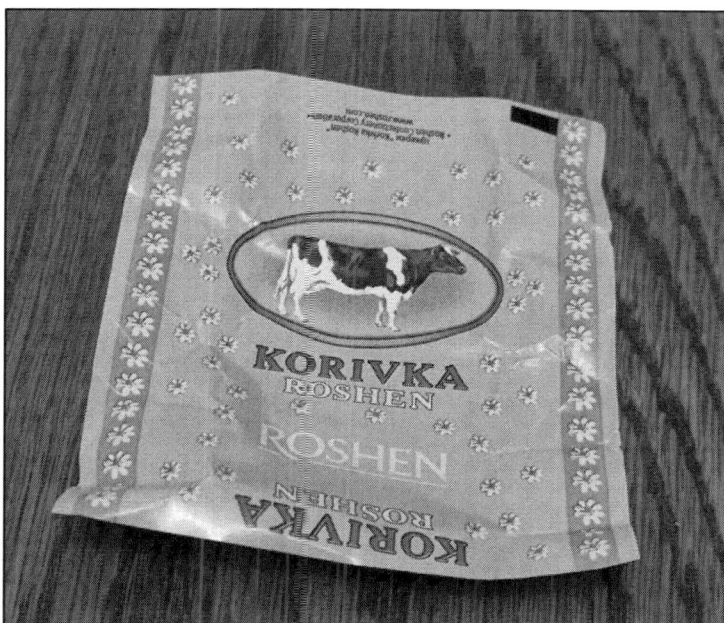

By the way, the brand is called **"the little cow "**in another language.

And isn't it peculiar how the cow on the packaging is looking in the exact same direction as the real cow by the water? If this didn't blow your mind yet, I don't know what will. But let's keep reading!

An exciting part of her story stood out to me.

She was explaining to her friends on that riverside about a time when she was with a friend of hers in India near the water, and out of nowhere, a cow bull started chasing them. **They got attacked!** That is crazy!

She emphasized how **scared** she was. And that they had to climb a tree to escape! But as she said that, **suddenly,** a large herd of cows appeared behind them and went to the water. **Two dozen cows** just casually passing by, very, very close.

Holy Cow, right?!

She was understandably shaken once again by the experience. All her friends were absolutely baffled and silenced by the experience They were unable to understand what just happened and how. How can something like that happen? They were in total **disbelief.** What happened to them is absolutely extraordinary! You just **can't explain these things away.**

How is this possible? How do things like that happen when they have close to zero chances to occur? And they happen over and over again, and **many people experience them** all around the world.

So, what is the driving force of this **mysterious mechanism?**

I want to present one last story that **will make your jaw drop!**

The following events happened to a close friend of mine.

The Bicycle and the Motherboard

One day, he received a letter from Slovenia in the mail. It revealed that he had an unknown inheritance there. He was perplexed for days. He didn't think too much of it.

For the story to make sense for you, you should know that he is also a computer and retro video game enthusiast and loves buying things online.

So one day, he was inspired to build a new computer for himself. He searched the Internet and came across a super rare, retro computer part at an **auction**. Something so rare that he used the expression, "the best in the world ever made, for my old enthusiast build." He quickly found himself in a **bidding war** for the rare part.

Luckily, he won and paid for that unique piece 1/5 of its worth! He explained how he felt a huge **adrenaline rush** when he seen that he won that rare computer part.

Right after that intense bidding battle, he felt like **going for a walk** outside and maybe doing some pull-ups, too. It was very late, around midnight, when he passed by the dumpster, and saw **two bicycles** right next to it. He was curious enough to take a closer look. He likes bicycles, too, and sometimes builds unique parts into them. The newfound bikes were old and dirty. Regardless, he decided to take home one of them.

Do you remember the computer part I mentioned before? Later in our conversation. he explained that the brand of that auction-won item, which happened to be a motherboard, is **ROG**. For me, that doesn't ring a bell. I know nothing about computers. So I kept on listening.

When he cleaned the bicycle at home, something hidden was revealed. Letter-by-letter words appeared out of the dust. **ROG**, it spelled. A so: **Ljubljana (Slovenia).**

He was in absolute disbelief! Immediately, my jaw dropped too! **I never heard a more captivating and so richly layered synchronicity story in my life!**

Let's attempt to summarize what happened in the last few pages: Here is a regular guy who has some inheritance going on in Slovenia. He goes into a bidding war for a retro computer motherboard branded **ROG.**

Then he goes outside right after that to have a walk, get some fresh air, and do some pull-ups. The very next thing that happens is he finds a bicycle in the dumpster with ROG and Ljubljana (Slovenia) written all over it!!!

This is crazy! This is beyond explainable. **A multi-layered synchronicity unfolded right in front of his eyes.** But what happened?

Clearly, it was a **manifestation**. But how?

How did this happen, and **why?**

He was experiencing heightened emotions during the bidding, including **excitement**, as **adrenaline** pumped through his body.

Nervousness: what if he doesn't win that unique part he stumbled upon?

Then, **happiness**, **relief**, and **euphoria** as he won the item! A massive rush of energy filled every cell of his body.

Did his emotions manifest the bicycle?

Did he want a bicycle? No. As far he knows. But then, **what's the explanation?**

An emotional high happened, and then things **manifested.**

That's all we know.

But why ROG? Why a bicycle? Why Slovenia?

It's a mechanism we barely grasp. But we are conscious witnesses.

Is it **magic?** Is it **science?** Could it be **both?**

As I write these lines, headlines emerged about the possibility that the **Sun is conscious.** Perhaps astrologers were right to call planets conscious entities, after all.

There is just so much **we don't know or understand** about our planet and about **the universe.**

But for a moment, let's say that the Sun is conscious. Let's assume that not only all the planets are conscious too, but the entire universe we live in. Perhaps a **superconscious.**

Manifestation stories tend to have one thing in common: an underlying **emotional charge** that we don't know how to *operate, control, or direct.*

It's just happening, and we are only the witnesses.

So what if our emotions are the very things that fuel manifestation?

*What if **the super-conscious responds** directly to our emotions?*

Let's try to explain it using science!

His **RAS,** his mammalian brain, focused on something he liked. That computer part, that **unique find.** That's a novelty about something you really love. **Novelty** means new information, a new experience.

Then, a huge **emotional charge** occurred during a very exciting bidding battle. Then, all he did was change his environment by **movement and action.** He went for a walk. That's all that happened until right before the moment he saw the bicycles.

We can see elements in this story that make the mammalian brain filter for what you want: **novelty**, which creates the most **focus**, and **emotion**, which makes it meaningful. Is that the magic equation?

These aren't isolated events. Many people have experienced similar phenomena before. But the question remains: How can we tap into this mysterious power and create the life we have always dreamed of?

So we must ask some important questions about his story:

What made him go for a walk? What made him pass by the dumpster? What made him take one of the bikes home and not the other?

How on earth did the ROG Ljubljana bicycle appear in that dumpster at the exact time when he won an auction for a "ROG"-branded motherboard?

Is it truly only the RAS at work?

Can it influence our decision-making processes, **inspire us to go for walks, look inside dumpsters, and take home things** from them?

How this was possible remains a mystery, but you can see that emotional charge seems to **manifest things out of thin air.**

So I can't help but wonder: what if we decided to use it for what we actually want?

What if we tried to replicate this process to manifest what we desire? Because no, **we don't hurt anyone by being happy.**

What if this is how we can **crack the code of reality?** What if we can manifest things we wish to experience or have on a daily basis? Wouldn't it be amazing? We can use this mysterious mechanism to our advantage! Even without understanding everything about it. Because here is the thing: The entire chain of events happened in as little as **an hour!**

Can you imagine what could happen if we decided to consciously use our emotions and our focus on a daily basis, and not just witness them and feel them? What if we can leverage this and experience its benefits **24/7**?

I believe we could. I believe we can **move mountains** and create the dreams we long for. And this book is here to help you **get to that summit!**

So let's explore what these stories have in common! It's not luck. And not only timing. **It's raw emotional charge: movement and action.**

These moments weren't planned, but they weren't passive either. Something shifted on the inside of people, and the outside **world responded.**

It mirrored back your internal reality.

That hidden element of every moment of magic:

So emotion, intensity, movement, and spontaneity seem to move the needle.

But what if you didn't have to wait for one of those moments to find you? **What if you could create them?** What if synchronicity didn't have to be a happy accident... but something you could spark on purpose?

That's exactly what we're going to explore next. But before that, let's summarize what we learned in this chapter.

Why This Changes Everything

So it's not that you failed to manifest; you just didn't know about the powerful elements that work behind the scenes.

Your Reticular Activating System has been waiting for you to focus and get emotional about it.

The moment you shift what your brain thinks is important, the world starts showing up differently, and **synchronicities flood your reality.**

Your old affirmations didn't fail because you're broken. They failed because they lacked real emotions.

Your vision board didn't miss because you're unlucky. It missed because you weren't in it.

So focus, emotional intensity, and action seem to be the keys. **The holy trinity of manifestation** that actually gives physical results. (as we have seen in those mind-blowing stories before).

But now, let's go ahead and explore synchronicities even more closely before we get into the concept of Impact Rap in Chapter 3.

Ready to dive in? **Let's go!**

CHAPTER 2

Synchronicity

• • •

*"Until you make the unconscious conscious, it will
direct your life and you will call it fate."*

— Carl Jung

We can undoubtedly say that all those people in the stories before have experienced synchronicities. But what is a synchronicity?

Swiss psychologist **Carl Jung** introduced the concept to describe meaningful coincidences that seem to be connected by more than chance. He explained that these events have no obvious link but feel **deeply significant** and, oddly, often **appear at the perfect moment.**

But why do they happen? **What's causing them?** Do they have something to do with the RAS? Or it's something purely spiritual? What is the answer?

What if they are the checkpoints in a rally that show you the map of what you manifest? Kind of like **signposts, signaling what's happening inside of you.**

And what about intuition? Isn't that supposed to be the ultimate internal compass?

Let's see!

The Comparison

First, we must know what they are to compare them. So, now that we know what synchronicity is, let's define intuition.

Here is what the search engine says:

Intuition (noun): The ability to understand or know something immediately, without the need for conscious reasoning or logical analysis.

Intuition is a sense we have that we cannot explain. Sometimes, things feel right, and sometimes, they just feel wrong. And more often than not, we can say that **listening** to our intuition is probably a good idea.

Have your intuition told you not to do something because it **just feels off**, but you ignored it, did it anyway, and the outcome was pretty bad? Well, we all did. We don't like to admit it, but we all have our own examples when it warned us but was left ignored.

So it seems that intuition is trying to **keep us on a path**, whether that's a safe path, the right path, or whatever path. It looks like it's another **mechanism** that we can feel and sense. One that warns us or makes us feel like we can go ahead, because it's safe to do so without harm.

On the other hand, **synchronicity** is a **feedback loop** that *appears in the outside physical world, like a mirror,* helping you to be aware of your internal mechanisms at work.

So we can say that it is something happening on the outside, while intuition is inside us, or at least that is our experience. But let's go deeper into the **rabbit hole!**

So there is intuition, synchronicity, and there is our **mind!** We are part of something **bigger than us** that is beyond our comprehension. We can perceive things that can help us make better decisions. We can see things in our physical reality that seem to connect meaningfully, but in ways we deem almost impossible. And we have a human mind! A **supercomputer** that still holds many mysteries to this day. Is the mind a creator, a receiver, a converter, a filter, or all of them at once?

Do we create thoughts, or do we perceive them?

And if we perceive them, then **we receive them.** Are we on the receiving end or the other?

It often feels like "our "thoughts **coming out of nowhere,** so either someone or something sends them, or we unconsciously download them from a big collective **super-connected,** perhaps from a **super-conscious "soup. "** Like "fishing out "a letter "A" from your tomato soup!

We have some fascinating mysteries surrounding us and existing within. It is only logical to assume that these mechanisms perhaps **rule our lives;** it's just that we don't understand how.

But why are we talking about synchronicities?

Because they are manifestations that came from us somehow. **We were inevitably part of it.**

But what drives the mechanism of manifestation? We all tried flat emotionless affirmations before, and they didn't work, so it's safe to assume that thoughts alone, or spoken words perhaps, are not the primary drivers of it.

But there is something to be said about spoken words:

It is my observation that they are very powerful. But here is the **catch!** Not if you have internal opposition to what you are saying. So if there is **any resistance** towards the words you speak, whether you know it or it's subconscious, it doesn't really matter, because **it will sabotage your attempts to manifest with affirmations.**

So, the most probable drivers of manifestation have to be INTENTION and EMOTION.

They somehow have power that breaks through barriers that spoken words just can't. Whatever the reason may be. So you see now that it's critical to **supercharge** your manifestation method with **emotions**. But what about the **intention** element of the equation?

It is a **collection of emotions and thoughts** that build up a complex experience and coherently point in a specific direction.

Okay! That's enough explaining for now! We have some serious substance to work with.

We learned what synchronicity is and how it compares to our intuition. We understood what intentions are.

What if we decided to set out for an **adventure** that combines them all?

Here is a unique approach to experience it for yourself!

A synchronicity walk!

Synchronicity Walk

Never heard of it? No problem!
This is how it works:

All you're going to do is walk, so don't worry too much about it right now.

First, you need to set an **intention**. Think of something you're curious about or need guidance on, like a question or a theme. It doesn't need to be super detailed. A simple **thought is enough.** It can be anything.

Here are some examples: It can be as simple as thinking of birds, books, or the idea of love, but you can be more specific, like *"Reveal what I'm not seeing in my life "*or *"Show me what I need to see/know."*

Then all you are going to do is start walking. There is **no logic,** no specific directions; just let your feet take you. It's actually a bit of an **intuitive walk,** because we let our inner guidance system take us for a stroll while we look out for synchronicities. So, truly, it's a hybrid of them. The key is not to have a plan or a fixed destination. Let your feet take you on a **quest!**

But let's turn it up a notch!

This part will require you to be connected to your intuition! After you set your intention, take any items, big or small, that you feel like taking with you on the walk!

May it be a small crystal, a sticker, a hand-written note, a book, or anything else. However silly it may be. You might feel guided to give them away during the walk or to leave it somewhere.

Life can surprise you in amazing ways. Pay attention to what you feel like wearing. Whether it's specific shoes, a jumper, or any other piece of clothing or accessories, **wear it,** even if it feels out of place. You never know who will initiate a conversation with you because of it.

As you walk, stay alert to things that **stand out.** Maybe it's a word or a sign, a number that keeps popping up, or a random conversation you overhear. These might seem random, but keep paying attention, as they could be meaningful. **Follow your nudges.** If you feel drawn to turn a certain way, enter a shop, or start a conversation yourself, trust that instinct and **go with it.**

Expect the unexpected.

A stranger's words, a song playing nearby, or an unusual sight might come your way. They can hold valuable messages for you. Stay open and engage with them **if you feel like it.**

How do you know that meeting a random stranger during a synchronicity walk isn't going to be the person who changes your entire life? How do we know that if only we were more authentic, wore the things we felt like wearing, and behaved in ways we knew deep down we wanted to, it wouldn't create a moment, a meeting, that would **revolutionize our existence?**

Making authentic choices in alignment with your inner truth is more important than you have ever been told.

In chapter 11, we will explore that topic further!

So, what do you do after a synchronicity walk?

Once you feel like your walk is over, all that's left to do is to go home and journal about your experience.

Did something interesting happen, or odd, or **significant?** What was it? Were there repeating numbers? Did a stranger give you something, tell you something, or show you something? Or even point you in a specific direction? Did some patterns emerge during the walk? Whatever you can collect and recall about this unique experience, **write it down! Because it can change your life!**

You're going to do great! Just enjoy it!

Now, let's summarize what we learned in this chapter.

What's Really Going On Here?

Synchronicity isn't luck. It's feedback, the universe responding to you in real time. Nodding back at you, "I heard you." Synchronicity is how life shows you what you're aligned with, or when something big just got triggered.

From now on, instead of waiting for the next mind-blowing moment to happen, you're equipped to spark them **on purpose.** And with intention. That's **powerful!**

Are you ready to discover the method that can finally yield results and turn past failures into **potent breakthroughs?**

In Chapter 3, we'll dive into Impact Rap! What it is, why it works better than anything you've tried before, and how to start using it today.

Imagine stepping into your future self in thought, movement, rhythm, and voice. Imagine embodying your dream life so vividly that your brain starts treating it as ***reality.*** *That's what's coming next!*

If you want real results, you don't just need to think differently. You need to manifest differently. And we're going to start **now.** It's time to revolutionize the way you create your reality! **Let's jump!**

CHAPTER 3

What Is Impact Rap? The Method That Works Better, Faster, And Stronger

● ● ●

"Words are, of course, the most powerful drug used by mankind."

— Rudyard Kipling

We discovered why traditional Manifestation techniques often fall flat. You now understand that your brain is already filtering everything, and you just have to train it to notice the right things. But here's the thing: knowing isn't enough.

Information without action is useless.

What if there was a way to fully activate your **RAS**, engage your entire body in the manifestation process, and supercharge with emotional intensity to **make it work?** What if there was a method that not only made you think about your dream life but also made you step into it, feel it, and live it in the now? That's exactly what **Impact Rap** does.

This isn't just about rhyming words or catchy lines. It's a full-body ritual that rewires your brain, anchors your vision in emotion, and **fires up your entire nervous system** to move.

This is Manifestation Revolution!

It's time to explore it for yourself!

What Is Impact Rap?

To unpack this new concept, first, let's examine what rap music excels at and how Impact rap got its name.

We all know some rap music lyrics, at least a line or two. They tend to get into our heads and never leave. They are **sticky!** And that's exactly what we need when thinking of manifestation. **You want your vision and mantras to stick like a rap song would.** But what makes them so powerful?

Rap music's rhythmic structure, dynamic delivery, and emotionally charged content can **influence the RAS better than anything!** So, when we engage with rap lyrics that speak to our values and desires, we **activate** the RAS in a way that makes us more likely to internalize those lyrics and act on their message. Emotionless affirmations and flat, generic vision boards completely lack this **intensity**.

So why the name Impact Rap? And what is it anyway?

It probably isn't what you think it is. It isn't music, and it's not traditional rap, either. It's not passive journaling, repeating words into a mirror, or quietly hoping for a better life. Impact Rap is much more powerful than that!

It got its name because, similarly to rap, it impacts the RAS in a unique way that we can leverage for manifestation. Its essential elements are **rhythm** and rhyme. It's a **revolutionary** method for bringing your dream life into your reality as quickly as possible.

So now, let's unpack this concept!

Impact Rap is a full-body, immersive method that fuses rhythm, rhyme, spoken words, visualization, and embodiment to rewire your brain for **success**. It combines three critical elements that most manifestation techniques miss:

- **Rhythm and Repetition:** That has the power to embed your vision deep into your subconscious mind.

- **Emotion and Energy** create a physical response that convinces your brain it's already happening. Emotion is the RAS **super-activator.**

- **Action and Expression:** Aligns your mind, words, and body to bridge the gap between wanting and doing.

So unlike affirmations, which often feel forced and surface-level, **Impact Rap turns your vision into a living, breathing experience.** You're not just stating your desires; you're acting them out, bringing them to life with rhymes and rhythm. Every word becomes emotion in motion. It becomes a masterful **manifestation mechanism.**

So, Let's Look at Why Impact Rap Works When Traditional Manifestation Methods Fail.

There's a reason why this new concept is so powerful. Rhythm, rhyme, and emotion don't just make words flow better, but more importantly, **they make them stick in your mind,** just like the last time a song got stuck in your head.

Or think about how easily a particular track can instantly bring back emotions or a **memory**. That's because rhythm and sound **activate multiple parts of your brain at once.**

It's not just about saying something. It's about experiencing it vividly in your mind. When words are assigned rhythm and emotion, they sink in much deeper, and become groundbreaking tools for **changing your reality**.

It's immersive. It's primal. It's neurological.

Impact Rap hijacks the brain's default mode and replaces it with your desired identity. It doesn't just talk to your conscious mind, it drills into your subconscious like a melody you can't forget.

It adds a **unique** layer that's rarely found in other manifestation techniques: **neural entrainment through rhythm.**

Now, Let's Compare Impact Rap to Different Manifestation Styles You Probably Tried Before, Based on Their Neurological Impact:

- Flat, generic affirmations *("I am successful")* → **very low impact.** Most people feel no emotional connection, so the brain ignores them.

- Written affirmations → **low impact.** Writing engages the motor cortex, reinforcing the idea slightly better. But not nearly enough to get serious results.

- Spoken rhythmic affirmations *(Impact Rap)* → **medium impact.** Rhythm activates Broca's and Wernicke's areas, the parts of your brain that tie language to deeper cognitive processing. **Now we're talking!**

- High-energy, emotionally charged, rhythmic Impact Rap → **high impact.** Emotional intensity triggers the limbic system, making words deeply ingrained and **highly activating** for your mind.

Can We Do Even Better?

You might be wondering how much more powerful impact rap could get. Supercharged spoken words are powerful. They shift emotions, reshape beliefs, and change how you see the world. But what if you didn't just say them, but truly stepped into a **vivid vision** of your desires **as you said them?**

Now, think about something you want. Something real, something you truly **desire** and feel deeply connected to.

And, instead of just explaining it, **let's step into it!**

It's full immersion!

We are connecting sounds, sensations, vision, emotions, and smells to rhythm and rhyme!

We are going to combine impact rap to a hyper-immersive visualization!

This is where it gets **fire.**

Are you ready?

Here is an excellent example of an immersive visualization:

You're in your campervan. The door creaks open, and fresh air rushes in. You feel the fabric of the seat beneath you, and the engine's hum as it comes to life.

You are looking ahead as the road stretches forward. You feel the breeze through the window; the sun warms your skin through the windshield.

Feel and see everything; it's like **the vision board of your dreams coming alive.** Now, put elements into this experience that you wish to have in your life.

Feel the **freedom** that you always wanted to have. Feel how liberating it is when your income streams are working for you behind the scenes while you live your dreams.

Feel the **excitement** of possibilities that life effortlessly presents to you. Feel the relief of knowing that **you are taken care of.**

Feel that captivating moment that calls you to act according to your values, to live out your **passions**, and to explore the world through that lens.

Enjoy that **you can do anything!** It's now in your power to be of service in a way that feels authentic and better than anything you did before.

Now, you start driving that camper-van in your vision with this incredible feeling flowing through your body. Choose your destination. What will you do there?...and so on.

Remember, this was only an example so you can understand what your visualization should be like. It should include **sensations, visuals, emotions, sounds, and even smells.**

Now let's see an example of a not-so-great, undetailed visualization:

I sit in the car, I drive into town, and I will build my dream tree house sometime.I feel kinda tired, but whatever, here i go.

What is wrong with it?

It's very flat and unemotional; it doesn't engage the senses or induce emotions. The vision is also disconnected because he is already building the tree house after going to town. But where are the supplies? We are missing many crucial details and many important parts of the vision.

You need to get into micro details as if you were rendering a video game in your mind!

Now let's take it up a notch and look at an even more amazingly detailed vision:

I can feel **my hands touch the leather** of the steering wheel in my car. Oh, it's a beautiful day! The sun radiates through the car and warms my skin. I breathe deeply, and the engine roams awake!

I hit the road and **feel the burning desire** in my bones to create something today! I pass by lush woodlands, and all I think of is the tree house I will build today. I can see the layout; it's amazing! I feel so powerful now! **I can do anything!**

Oh, I can see the lumberyard! I have arrived! I stop the car, and I jump out! **I can smell the lumber.** What a heavenly scent! I soak it into my cells.

I walk to the piles that cover the yard left and right. **I touch the wood** and run my fingertips down its surface. This is perfect. **This will be my house, I say to myself, smiling...** and so on.

This is how detailed your visualization should be to have tangible results! But you can go much deeper than that, of course! You could say that birds are sitting on the lush woodland trees you passed by. You can get extremely detailed about the lumber and its texture, the different colors, and the smells. This could go on for pages and pages.

You can even have a specific outfit in your vision that you always wear in this scenario, which somehow makes you feel connected to your dreams.

Let me clarify that: an outfit that you wear in your vision is great, but wearing it in real life while doing this exercise is **masterful!**

Your vision must be super detailed not only to be effective but also to create a fertile ground for your impact rap, as it will become the basis of it.

So, we are talking about three elements here:

1. A very detailed written vision that you are able to visualize with no problem and **no inner resistance.**

2. A super effective impact rap that is descriptive of your vision but is infused with rhythm and rhyme.

3. A dedicated vision board for your visualization.

Now, let's explore what a low-performing and high-performing impact rap would look like for the same vision!

Let's start with the high-performing one!

Get ready! This will knock your socks off!

DREAM TREE HOUSE RAP-High Impact

(Verse 1)

Rollin' down the street, hands grip the wheel,

Sunlight beamin', yeah, this vibe is real.

Engine wakes up, hear that roar,

Got a dream to build, can't wait no more!

Burnin' inside, got that fire in my bones, "

A vision so clear, man, I see it like a throne!

Passin' by trees, yeah, I see my fate,

A treehouse palace—man, I just can't wait!

(Chorus)

Ohh, I'm a build it high, up in the sky, ""'

My dream, my castle, I'm a watch it rise!

Feelin' so strong, yeah, I own today,

Ain't nothin' stoppin'—get up out my way!

(Verse 2)

Hit the lumberyard, yeah, I'm steppin' out,

Wood so fresh, gotta breathe it down! "

Inhale deep, let it soak my soul,

A builder's dream, yeah, I'm in control!

Stacks on stacks, wood left and right,

I run my fingers down—this feelin's right!

"This is my house," yeah, I whisper low,

Brick by brick, watch this kingdom grow!

(Chorus)

Ohh, I'm a build it high, up in the sky,

My dream, my castle, I'm a watch it rise!

Feelin' so strong, yeah, I own today,

Ain't nothin' stoppin'—get up out my way!

(Bridge)

Saw in my hand, let's cut that beam,

Hammer in the other—yeah, live my dream!

Nail by nail, every board I place,

Turnin' this wood to my dream escape!

(Outro)

Ain't just a house—this a legacy,

A place that'll last for eternity.

Blood, sweat, dreams—I put it all in,

Yeah, my dream house, man, let's begin!

DROP THE MIC—IT'S BUILDING TIME!

I told you this would knock your socks off!
Now let's look at the one that won't get you results.

DREAM TREE HOUSE RAP-Low Impact

(Verse 1)

Drove my car, now I'm here,

Sun is bright, sky is... clear?

Gonna build, yeah, it'll be tall,

With, uh... wood and maybe a wall.

(Chorus)

Oh, yeah, this house is good,

Made of stuff... mostly wood.

Has a roof, or maybe not,

Uh... forgot what else I got.

(Verse 2)

Hammer go tap, nails go in,

This is my house, I'm gonna win!

Floor is down, walls are... too?

Yeah, I think I'm almost through.

(Outro)

House is done, yeah, I'm proud,

Wait... where's the door? Oh well....the end.

I hope you got the joke!

So now you can see that this isn't just imagination. It is a super powerful, life-changing method. Your brain records all of it and believes it fully. If you do it right, this visualization and impact rap combination rushes your dream life to you.

It's a method that rewires your brain to expect **THAT** reality. The more vividly you engage with it, the more **inevitable** it becomes.

The goal of this book is to create a visualization filled with what you truly, deeply want, things that are most meaningful to you, combined with lyrics that have rhythm and rhyme.

Match your impact rap lyrics to the scene's evolution as you visualize. Say them out loud as the scenes change in your mind. **Match your impact rap lyrics in real time to how your visualization flows.**

You can create as many impact raps as you wish, but focus on quality over quantity. Don't worry if you have only one. What's important is that **it works.**

The secret is to have a vision board for each of your visions and visualizations individually. So, to clarify, you don't just make a vision board for your dreams like you've seen it all over social media.

We are going micro here! **Your visualizations need a dedicated vision board** filled with visions, scenes, and all the essential and significant elements of your visualization scene.

Do everything in your power to find or create images and photos that perfectly radiate **the scene and the emotions** and sensations that your visualization is all about, because **THAT will change your life!**

So, if you want a car, don't just imagine that car; imagine the feelings and sensations of being inside that car. Collect pictures that represent not only the car but also the emotions of how that feels.

Anything that induces that same feeling inside you has the right to make it to the vision board. In fact, It's a must!

*The moment your mind fully accepts your vision as real, without any resistance, everything in your life starts to shift in ways **you never imagined possible.***

Why Are We Doing This?

When you combine rhythm, emotion, and detailed and exceptionally vivid visualization, your brain doesn't know the difference between reality and mental rehearsal. Studies show that mental rehearsal can improve real-life performance by up to **45%. Athletes** do this before competitions, and their muscles fire as if they're practicing. Your brain primes your body, emotions, and actions as if your new reality is already happening.

So why do people hesitate to act if their brain and body are activated 100%?

It's because the subconscious mind still has resistance, layers of *doubt, and fear.* The moment you work through them, things will start to shift rapidly. **When you immerse yourself fully in words, rhythm, emotion, and visualization, you're hacking past that resistance.**

This is the absolute key to your successful manifestation! **You can override old mental scripts** much faster. You're not just hitting the threshold of change; you're **breaking through the barriers that kept you stuck.**

You don't have to force manifestation or obsess over results anymore. You just have to activate your brain so powerfully with what you want, that your decisions, actions, and energy naturally will pull them into your reality like **you have your own gravity.**

How to Use Impact Rap to Manifest Your Dream Life

The best way to understand it is to try it. Here's a very brief step-by-step breakdown of how impact rap is created. Later in the book, we'll explore each step in depth in the coming chapters.

Step 1: Define Your Vision – Create Your Written Visualization

Close your eyes. Picture your future self. It's not just an image. You have to feel it. Where are you? What do you see? **What are you doing and why?** Are there any significant parts of that vision? What are they? How does it feel to have what you desire? Get very specific; feel it with all your senses because this is where the magic happens!

Step 2: Turn It Into Rap Lyrics

Let's transform that vision into **rhythmic lyrics** that flow and rhyme like real rap.

For example:

> I am thriving, I'm strong and free,
>
> My success comes to me.
>
> I wake up happy, my path is clear,
>
> Oh my god, my dream life is here!

Rhyming is required, as it helps lock in the rhythm, making it easier to recall and repeat with emotion.

Step 3: Speak It with Power

Stand up. Breathe deep. Speak your Impact Rap out loud, **with conviction!** Don't just say the words, **FEEL THEM.** Move if you want to. Gesture. Act as if you are already living it. Notice how your body reacts. How does it feel? Do you feel a shift? A surge of confidence? **A surge of energy or joy?** That's your brain responding to the embodiment of your vision. **Right now, it believes it to be true.**

Step 4: Repeat Daily & Adjust as Needed

The more you do this, the stronger the **neural pathways** in your brain become. **Repetition is key.** Adjust your Impact Rap to reflect your next-level goals as you grow and evolve.

That's the formula. But what if you skip it?

What If You Don't Do This?

Let's discuss what happens when you don't fully commit to manifesting with impact rap and stick to the same old passive methods.

Your RAS remains programmed to filter out opportunities. You'll keep missing signs, connections, and breakthroughs because your mind isn't trained to recognize them.

Your subconscious stays in "wishful thinking" mode. Without emotional engagement, your dreams remain fantasies instead of reality.

You keep running in circles. Saying "I am successful" without believing won't shift your identity or actions.

The choice is yours.

Keep doing what hasn't worked, or **step into something new** that forces your mind and body to align with your desired future.

So... Why Is Impact Rap a Game-Changer?

You're not here to whisper wishes into the void!

You're here to **rewire your brain.**

To move. To speak. To *become conviction.*

Impact Rap isn't just clever rhyming. **It's neuroscience in motion.** Rhythm, emotion, and repetition together ignite your **RAS** activation.

And that's when your brain starts treating your vision like *reality.* You start embodying it *loud enough for the universe to echo back.* Suddenly, it's not "I hope."

It's **"I'm living it."**

You're not just saying you're free; you're *feeling the wheel in your hands, the road beneath you, and the sun on your skin.* **You are living your best life!**

That's exactly what I want you to experience!

So, next, I will teach you how to build a **powerful Impact Rap library** that you can use anytime, anywhere, to fuel your growth and transformation.

It's time to take your life to the next level.
Are you ready?

CHAPTER 4

Different Types Of Impact Rap Tailored To Every Area Of Life

• • •

"The way we talk to ourselves matters. Our words shape our reality."

— Lisa Nichols

By now, you know how to craft a **powerful statement** that activates your RAS and aligns your mind and body with your vision. But manifestation isn't a one-size-fits-all.

How you manifest financial freedom isn't the same as manifesting deep, fulfilling relationships or a stronger, healthier body.

It's time to **expand your toolkit!**

Just like you wouldn't wear the same shoes for every occasion, you cannot use the same Impact Rap for every aspect of your life. It probably wouldn't fit.

You need a customized arsenal of powerful, high-energy statements that match the specific goals you're working toward.

In this chapter, we'll explore how to tailor your lyrics to any part of your life, no matter what you wish to experience.

Let's get started!

1. The Fitness & Energy Impact Rap

What It Is: This type of Impact Rap is perfect for you if you wish to improve your **well-being** and health with movement. It could push you beyond barriers where you would have quit before and help you break mental resistance during your workouts. It could override the voice that says, *"I can't"*. If done right, it can fortify your mind to push through, **keep going, and achieve.** The stronger your mind, the stronger your body.

Have you ever noticed that working out isn't just physical? **It's mental,** too! The hardest part isn't lifting the weight or running the mile. **It's convincing yourself to keep going when your mind tells you to quit.**

Impact Rap can be your **mental pre-workout.** It could shift you into a high-energy state and a mindset that makes you unstoppable. That is a big deal!

Get your **journal** and start writing down lines that feel authentic to your vision. Create your powerful fitness rap lyrics with conviction. Make it rhyme, give it rhythm, and make it so good **it gets you moving!**

Before any workout session, stand tall and say your crafted impact rap. Or during a workout or in between sets.

But for now, here is an example:

My body is strong, my mind is fire,

Every word flies me higher.

I train with power, I push with speed,

I have the power and the strength I need.

Do you feel that? This isn't just motivation; it's programming your brain to expect **strength** and **resilience.** If you do it right, you will feel pumped after saying it!

The important part is that you craft it to suit your **needs** and perfectly match your **personal fitness vision!**

2. The Dream Life Impact Rap

What It Is: This type of Impact Rap shifts you into gear! It's all about the identity of your future self, the version of you who already lives your dream. It could help erase self-doubt and align you with confidence, clarity, and success. **The more you embody this energy, the faster your dream life unfolds.** This is about stepping into your vision NOW, not waiting for *"someday."*

Have a vision for your life. A version of yourself that is **thriving, fulfilled,** and living out your purpose with confidence. Step into that version of yourself **right now!**

Most people wait. They think, one day, when I have more money, more time, more clarity... then I'll live my dream, then I'll make them happen, then I'll go after them. **That's the wrong approach.**

> **You don't wait for your dreams. You step into them NOW.**

Try This: Close your eyes and imagine your future self walking into the room. **Confident**. At peace. Overflowing with abundance.

Now say:

> I live my purpose; I walk in the light,
>
> My vision is strong, my future is bright.
>
> Opportunities flow, doors swing wide,
>
> I trust the journey; my life is golden!

Manifestation happens when you *act as if your future is already real.* It's all about experiencing how good it feels to live your vision. The more you can do that and embody it, the faster it **materializes.**

Here is a visual hack that can help you erase some barriers in your mind when it comes to the timeframe of your manifestation:

You are not pulling the future into reality, into the now. What happens when you start imagining your vision, is that **energy** inside your body starts to grow; it **radiates through you and beyond you** as you imagine the fine details of your vision with emotions and sensations.

This potent energy becomes your reality.

So, you are not pulling the future to you, but *creating it in real-time, right here, right now.*

This blurs the lines of time, with the future and the now becoming one. **It all becomes...NOW.** It's fascinating!

3. The Money & Abundance Impact Rap

What It Is: Money is deeply tied to subconscious beliefs. Unfortunately, if you think wealth is hard to earn, **you'll prove yourself right.** This type of Impact Rap could rewire your financial mindset, shifting you from scarcity to abundance. *It programs your brain to expect wealth,* **recognize opportunities,** and act like a person who naturally attracts financial success.

Money, as well as everything else, is energy. And if you've been programmed to believe that wealth is hard to come by, that success is reserved for *"lucky"* people, or that you're *"not the type"* to be financially free...guess what? That's exactly what your RAS will filter for you. You will only see struggle, scarcity, and limitations.

It's time to rewire your financial mindset.

So pick up a pen and start writing whatever comes, just like before, but now it's all about money! Say your tailor-made rap lyrics with confidence daily.

Here is a money rap example:

Money flows, wealth is near,

Abundance comes, I have no fear.

My value is high, my worth is clear,

I attract success; my time is here.

4. The Social, Friendship & Community Impact Rap

What It Is: Connection is everything. Whether you want deeper friendships, a robust network, or stronger relationships, this type of Impact Rap helps **you become a magnet** for meaningful interactions.

You attract people who align with your energy and vision by radiating confidence and authenticity.

Success means nothing if you have no one to share it with.

And if you've ever felt alone, disconnected, or that you can't attract the right people into your life, then your subconscious beliefs around relationships need **a shift.**

It's the perfect time to clarify your social vision and start writing it down.

If you need a best friend, **write it down!**

If you wish to attract a new social circle, **make that rhyme!** Give it all you got!

This is your new life!

Say your social rap before social events, networking, or any time you need to attract positive people.

Here is a social rap example:

> I am magnetic, I shine so bright,
>
> I attract my tribe; my soul feels light.
>
> The right connections find their way,
>
> Love and friendship always stay.

Remember: Your energy is a **beacon.** The stronger you believe in your worth, the more you attract people who are aligned with you.

5. The Resilience & Unstoppable Mindset Impact Rap

What It Is: Life will test you, but this type of Impact Rap can strengthen your ability to adapt, rise, and push through any challenge. It could help you build an unshakable mindset so **you don't break when obstacles appear;** you evolve. This is the Impact Rap for those who don't want to quit and are ready to own their path.

Life throws challenges at you, but you don't have to be at their mercy. Your ability to **adapt and keep going** is the difference between success and failure. It's for the days you feel like giving up, when doubt creeps in, and you need to remind yourself **who you are.**

How does it sound? Is it bold? Is it brave? Let's write it down! You know what to do.

But for now, you can try this:

I rise, I fight, I stand up strong,

No fear can shake me; I am strong.

I bend, but never will I break,

I own my path; I shape my fate.

When times get tough, repeat your mindset rap. Remind yourself how awesome you are! Your mind will follow.

Impact Rap for the Moments That Break You

Let's stop pretending life is all vision boards and a future you energy. What about the days when nothing lands? I'm talking about **heartbreak, rejection,** and **exhaustion.** *Loneliness* in a room full of people. Waking up and feeling like your chest is holding a collapsed building.

This is when *manifestation posts make you roll your eyes.* This is when you don't want a "positive mindset." You want to scream and disappear. You want to feel like something still makes sense. This is where **Impact Rap transforms into soul medicine.**

Not to fix you or push the pain away, but to give your soul a voice again. Sometimes, what you need is not a solution, but

a blank page on which you can spill your pain with ink.
A line that holds your truth so hard that you cry when you say it. You write it when your heart's still bleeding. You write it with shaky hands and swollen eyes. It no longer needs to rhyme, unless it feels right.

Here is an example of the rhyming version:

"I gave love with my whole damn chest,

and they dropped it like it was made of glass.

But I'm still here, full of fire and breath,

and I won't turn my heart to ash."

When you can write like that, that's **powerful.** You are reclaiming what was ripped out. *Maybe you were ghosted, betrayed, or left out.*

Here is your medicine:

"I saw the door slam in my face,

but still I stayed standing.

I'm done begging for space—

now I walk with high hopes and grace!"

This is how you become whole again!

Not by suppressing your emotions, but by transmuting them. But what about **burnout?** Let's talk about it. You've been running on fumes. You've said yes too many times. You're tired of trying to prove your worth, that you're enough. I feel you. **Pause. Breathe. Write it out.**

If you can't find the words, let me find them for you:

"I'm allowed to rest without guilt.

I've earned the stillness.

I don't hustle for my worth—

I return from the illness."

There's something sacred in speaking to your exhaustion with compassion. Not shaming yourself for slowing down, but honoring it like you whisper to your heart **"I hear you now."**

Impact Before Impact

What if you wrote an Impact Rap before something big? Before an interview. Before that date. Before the pitch, the confrontation, or the risk. Before you make the ask.

Do it. Get in front of the mirror. Get in your body. Don't wait until you feel confident! Speak until **confidence becomes your nature.** Let's try something!

Say these lines in front of the mirror with power and emotion:

> "I walk in grounded, I walk in clear,
>
> I don't chase—I draw near.
>
> My voice is calm. My truth is sharp.
>
> They feel me before I even start."

You're not pretending. You're programming. You're showing your nervous system what's about to happen so it doesn't flinch when it comes. If you do that enough, you'll realize you've been in charge the whole time.

You've always been the alchemist.

Your Personal Impact Rap Library

Now, you don't just have one Impact Rap; you have a whole set customized to your goals. Isn't that amazing? That is your *toolbox for transformation!*

All you need to do is *SAY THEM OUT LOUD. DAILY. WITH ENERGY AND EMOTION.*

So, What's in Your Toolkit Now?

This chapter was a full-body permission slip. Permission to **custom-build** the version of you that will live your dreams. But one Impact Rap won't cover it all. Because your money rap won't sound like your body goals. And **your dream life will require its own unique voice.**

So here's what we did:

We crafted a library filled with **fitness raps, money raps, dream-life anthems, resilience chants, and community magnets.** Now, your voice can meet every version of you that's ready to evolve.

You have also learned how to:

Speak before you're ready. Write from your pain, not bypass it. Because Impact Rap isn't just for the high moments. It's also for the heartbreaks, the breakdowns, the *"no more tears left to cry "*nights.

You've come out the other side!

Use your impact raps like your future depends on it.
Because it does.

Next Steps: Where the magic really happens

In Chapter 5, we'll explore advanced techniques, including crafting longer, more emotionally charged statements and combining them with strategic action to **accelerate results.**

This next part is where **it all comes together.** When you take what you've learned and craft something so powerful, it starts working for you the moment you say it.

Let's knock this out of the park!

Mastering Advanced Techniques

• • •

"Energy flows where attention goes."

— Tony Robbins

You already know the power lyrics have when you speak your Impact Rap with high energy and conviction.

But now, it's time to take things to mastery level.

We will reprogram your subconscious, shift your mindset, and accelerate your results.

Most people stay stuck in wishful thinking because they lack **intensity and action.** We will fix that right now!

This next level is about **precision**! How to craft, deliver, and embody your message so deeply that it becomes **automatic.** You'll learn to adjust your tone, breath, pace, and physicality for **maximum effect.** This is where your words stop being words and start becoming **commands to your nervous system.**

Let's go!

Step 1: Building More Emotionally Charged Impact Raps

A short Impact Rap is perfect for quick motivation, but when you start crafting longer, **more immersive raps,** you step deeper into the identity of the future version of yourself.

The more detailed the lyrics are, the more transformational power they carry.

Here's a step-by-step guide on how to elevate your impact rap to mastery level:

- **Start with Your Core Vision** – What's the **BIG** transformation you want? Get extremely clear. What is the vision that you want to materialize in your life?

- **Break It Down into Key Areas** – Career, health, finances, relationships, and mindset. Define what success looks like in each of these categories. You can't go wrong here. **Just do it!** Whatever floats your boat. What's important is that you **get clear and get it done.**

- **Add Descriptive, Emotionally Driven Language—** make it real and vivid. As you read in the example with the campervan, be vivid and detailed. **Involve all senses;** whatever feels good for you, make it come alive!

- Use Present & Future Tense – Speak as if it's already happening while **reinforcing what's coming.**

- Build Rhythm & Flow – The smoother and more natural your Impact Rap feels, the more powerfully **it programs your subconscious mind.**

Let me show you an example of a Longer Impact Rap:

I wake up clear, my mind is strong, I know my path, I can't be wrong. Doors swing open, my future is bright, I walk in purpose, I move in the light. Money flows easily, my impact is bold, I love my life!

Step 2: The Secret Element – Emotional Activation

As we know now, **words alone will never be enough.** Your **emotional state dictates** what sticks in your mind and what happens. Think about a time you learned a remarkable amount of things in a surprisingly short time. Do you remember your emotional state when that happened? Why do you think that was possible? **Emotions imprint experiences into your brain.** So, we need to utilize them in your impact rap.

Here is how to activate Emotions in Your Impact Rap:

- **Use Your Voice Dynamically** – Don't just say it, **OWN IT.** Speak with power, whisper if you want, and make it dramatic.
- **Move Your Body** – Stand up, walk around, gesture! Your brain connects movement with meaning. **Involve your whole body** in the experience as much as possible to the degree that it feels genuine and comfortable.
- **Use Facial Expressions** – When you say I am unstoppable, say it like you already won. **Feel it in your bones!**
- **Tie It to a Memory or Visualization** – Imagine the moment you achieve your dream as you speak. **This is everything!**

Step 3: Make Yourself Unstoppable With Action

Speaking your vision-fueled impact rap with conviction is a game-changer already! But here are some **pro tips to start changing your life today:**

- **Link Every Impact Rap to an Actionable Step.** After your impact rap-visualization session, what's one thing you can do today to move toward your vision? Do something small that aligns with your vision.

Remember, your brain needs proof.

- **Track Small Wins.** Because it loves progress too. The more you recognize your wins, **the stronger your belief will be**.

So celebrate them!

- **Pair Your Impact Rap with a Routine.** Speak it before a workout, before work, or before bedtime! **Make it part of your lifestyle.** Make it seamlessly fit.

Let me show you what Impact Rap can do in real life!

Impact Rap in Action: A Real-life Manifestation Story

It was a typical day, just another afternoon helping my father declutter his house. I was going through old things. But looking back, I wasn't just cleaning and organizing; I was making space for something new, physically and mentally.

I was standing in front of an old wardrobe. It had many different compartments, and I was curious to know **what mysteries it could hold.**

I opened the first drawer. You couldn't believe what was hiding in it. I found my **late grandmother's purse.** A wave of nostalgia hit me, and I teared up. I was hesitant to open it, but *my curiosity nudged me on.*

I expected to find nothing more than faded receipts or forgotten keepsakes. But to my biggest surprise an abundance of **cash was neatly tucked away in its pockets.** In every little part of it there was a *different currency!* Crisp, untouched bills and coins from places I'd never even been. I was blown away! How did I find such a thing?

I had been worrying about money, questioning my financial future, and feeling like abundance was always out of reach. But here it was, literally **in my hands.** And then I remembered.

The day before, I had written my very first
Impact Rap and declared out loud that money was
flowing to me and that it was no longer something I had
to chase; it was already finding its way into my life. I had
spoken those words **boldly, rhythmically, as if they
were already true.**

And now, standing there, staring at the unexpected
discovery, I felt something shift inside me. Suddenly,
things were possible, but more importantly, **I believed
them to be possible.** It was never about *"finding"*
money. It was about finally believing I can have it.

The money had always been there. I just haven't seen it.
That moment changed something more profound than
just my bank account. It changed the way I saw
everything.

What else was already waiting for me to see it? **What
opportunities had I been blind to** because I believed
they weren't there because my RAS wasn't filtering for
that kind of reality? I had spoken abundance into
existence, and reality responded. **This is real! I made
it happen! OMG!**

But now, I wonder, **what would happen when you
try it?** What would be the first thing you want to
manifest like you mean it? Let's review the steps and see
how to make it happen!

So What Did We Unlock Here?

You learned to supercharge your lyrics, deepen your vision, and let your **energy match your words.** This is how you close the gap between your dreams and your current life.

One line. One emotion. One belief at a time.

And the best part is that we're just warming up!

As we move into **Chapter 6,** we'll get to the *deepest parts of your soul.* We'll unearth your **core values, life purpose, and authentic vision.** You'll refine your Impact Raps to ensure they aligns with your essence. The stronger your **WHY** is, the more unstoppable you become.

It's time to lock in your real purpose! The only thing truly worth manifesting.

Let's go!

Find Your Purpose & Refine Your Vision

• • •

"Your purpose in life is to find your purpose and give your whole heart and soul to it."

— Buddha

You've come this far. You know how Impact Rap works. You've seen its power. You've crafted different Impact Raps for various areas of life by now. **You are amazing!**

But let's ask the ultimate question: *Are you* **100%** *sure your Impact Rap reflects your deepest truth and* **soul-level desires?** If there's even a shred of doubt, don't worry; you're exactly where you need to be.

This chapter is all about helping you find **clarity** about what really matters. Because if your Impact Rap isn't aligned with **your values and true purpose,** it won't stick, it won't ignite your soul, and it won't have **transformational power** in your life.

We'll refine, deepen, and sharpen your Impact Rap until it becomes *unshakable*, so personal, and so powerful that it moves you every single time you say it. We're going to create **authentic energy** here! It's time to remove the surface layers and uncover what truly drives you. Let's ask the hard **questions!**

So fasten your seatbelts. We're going for the stars!

Step 1: What Do You Truly Want? For Real!

Most people think they know what they want. More money. A better career. A thriving relationship. But when you strip it all down, when you remove the expectations, the pressure, the outside influences...**is that really what YOU want?** Take a moment. Sit with it.

And ask yourself:

1. What would I truly do with my life if **no one** had a say?

2. If money wasn't an issue, **what would get me out of bed** every day, because I would be so excited to do it?

3. What makes me feel so alive, that it feels like **I'm meant to do it?**

4. What moments in my life have given me the **deepest sense of meaning?**

5. If I had only one year left to live, what would I do with it? And **why are those things so important to me?**

Your Impact Rap needs to align with what matters **to you,** not what you think you're supposed to want or do. Pro Tip: **Don't filter your answers** to these questions. Write down whatever comes up, even if it seems unrealistic, silly, or scary, especially if it's scary.

Step 2: What's Been Holding You Back?

Now that you know what you truly want, let's examine the other side:

What's stopping you from pursuing it? Why haven't you done it already?

If you haven't achieved it yet, there must be something in the way. More often than not, the things stopping you aren't external circumstances but **your internal beliefs.**

So ask yourself:

- **What stories** have I been telling myself about why I can't have the thing I want?

- **What fears** arise when I think about stepping into this version of myself?

- **Where have I been playing small,** settling, or holding back? And Why?

- **What's the worst thing** that could happen if I go all in? Is that fear real? Is that the worst that can happen?

  Or is the worst thing that I never even tried?

- **Who would I be** if I let go of every excuse and just did the things I wanted?

This is about **awareness**. You can't break free from limiting beliefs unless you are aware of them, but once you are, you can **take away their power.**

Pro Tip: Look at your answers. Now, flip them. If you wrote, *"I'm not confident enough,"* re-frame it as *"I am growing into my most confident self right now."* Turn every limiting belief into an empowering one.

Then, do something to prove it right, so your brain has the proof it needs.

Step 3: What Are Your Core Values?

Your Impact Rap won't work if it's based on goals that don't align with your deepest values. If success means sacrificing what truly matters to you, you'll sabotage yourself before you ever get there.

So, let's dig deep enough to discover your core values:

1. What principles do **I refuse** to compromise on?

2. What kind of **impact** do I want to make in the world?

3. What kind of person do I want to be, not just what I want to achieve?

4. If my success didn't **FEEL right**, would I still want it?

5. What **values** do I want my impact rap to reflect?

6. What end goal do I wish to arrive at in my life?

Your purpose isn't just about what you do. It's about who you are. When your Impact Rap aligns with your values, it will feel natural, **it will feel right.**

Pro Tip: If you feel resistance toward some words of the lyrics, then you need to **rewrite them.** Ensure that all words and expressions of the lyrics reflect your deepest truths and authentic purpose. If there is any opposition or resistance, **it won't work.**

For example: If your impact rap lyrics say, „ *I'm running towards my goals,* " but it feels wrong to you because deep down, **it feels rushed,** and you would much rather say, „*I'm walking towards my goals,*" then definitely say that.

Make sure you are paying attention to every word, as **it must 100% align with who you are.**

If you are not willing to go below the surface, no method in the world can help you achieve the results you desire.

Step 4: Key Questions You Must Ask

Now we're switching gears, and focusing on the **authenticity** of your impact rap. Defining your vision is the foundation for writing rap lyrics that speak to you. So, let's make them even better! These questions ensure you can lock in **maximum impact** and **authenticity.**

What Do You Want Your Rap to Do for You?

The questions to ask yourself:

- *What is the purpose of this rap?*
- Is it to push through struggles, **build confidence,** or describe your goals?

The answers will shape the content and tone of your lyrics.

- If your rap is about overcoming barriers, you probably want to write about **resilience** and inner strength.
- The message might focus on **courage** and personal power if it reinforces self-belief.

Choosing Words That Resonate Is A Must!

Identify the words, emotions, and sensations that bring your rap to life.

- What words energize you?
- What words make you feel powerful?

- Which words best represent your vision?

- What words do you feel like using? Why?

This isn't about picking trendy **words**; it's about selecting the ones that **feel right.** If your rap is about transformation, words like *rise, unbreakable, or reclaim* might carry the energy you need. Think about how they make you feel when you say them.

- Do they feel too **average**, too **shallow**, to **surface level?**

- Do they ignite **excitement**, possibility, or **passion**?

Whichever ones feel right for you, write them down in your journal! **Does it fit?**

Ask yourself:

1. How do my lyrics connect to my vision? Do they? Does it even make sense?

2. How do they align with my purpose and values?

3. What action do I want them to inspire me to take?

Make sure you prioritize getting this right!

Your goal is to create lyrics that hit home with **emotional** and **motivational impact** so that they can propel you forward.

Step 5: The Final Refinement – Creating Your Ultimate Impact Rap

Now, with everything you've uncovered, let's craft the final, **most powerful version of your lyrics.**

- It must reflect what you **TRULY** want.

- It must address and **rewrite** your limiting **beliefs.**

- It must align with your **deepest values.**

- It must ignite something in you and make you feel **unstoppable**.

When you have your final version, **it's time to go all in!**

Say it out loud. Feel into it. If it doesn't hit deep, tweak it. Keep refining your lyrics until they **move you.**

If they don't, it's not good enough.

And it will do nothing for you.

I'm telling you this because I want you to rock it!

I want you to win!

Finding Who You Are and Saying It Out Loud

This chapter was all about finding your inner fire that **can't wait to light your way home.** To a place you have always dreamed of, to a life that finally feels right.

You've peeled back the layers that held you back from knowing. You've questioned what you didn't dare before. **It's a revolution**. And now your Impact Rap isn't just a rhythm. It's a revelation of who you are.

You stopped writing what sounded right and started saying what felt real. **Words you can stand for.** You're not manifesting from fantasy anymore. You're manifesting from **alignment.**

This chapter brought it full circle: your voice, vision, and values, all tuned to the same frequency. *Something clicked.*

In the next chapter, we'll dive into something that became so natural to us that we don't even notice its presence anymore. Can you guess what it is?

Of course it's **technology**.

We're about to untangle how it can help or hinder our manifestation. So, let's read ahead and immerse ourselves in **the network of possibilities.**

CHAPTER 7

Manifesting In The Digital Age How Tech Can Help Or Hinder You

● ● ●

"The real danger is not that computers will begin to think like humans, but that humans will begin to think like computers."

— Sydney J. Harris

We are more connected than ever. And more **distracted** than ever. We carry tiny portals in our pockets, feeding us inspiration, envy, **dopamine**, doubt, validation, and noise. All at once. All the time.

And when it comes to manifestation...this can be your greatest tool or your biggest block.

We live in the digital age, but you need to know how to **harness its power.**

Otherwise, it will **hijack** your life and energy *before you finish your morning coffee.*

Let's unpack it because it's not so black and white. Tech is not "bad." But the way you use it decides everything.

Because the algorithms aren't neutral. They're **trained to hijack your desire,** unless you flip the script and train them to serve your vision.

Your **phone** can distract you from your goals, or become a sacred altar. It can drain your **focus**, or serve as your most potent manifestation amplifier.

The choice is yours. Let's learn how to own it!

The Subtle Way Tech Destroys Manifestation

You're about to do your Impact Rap. You're finally in a focused state. You're feeling good, open, alive. Ready to embody your future self?

Then... **ping.**

A notification. Someone followed you. Someone liked your story. Someone posted something that **instantly takes your focus away.**

That one-second distraction just kicked you off course.

You're back in observer mode. You're not the creator anymore. You're the consumer once again.

And this is how most people live all day long.

You are not in manifestation energy anymore.

Your attention is **scattered**.

Your manifestations get choked at the roots, because your **RAS is constantly switching direction,** *influenced by someone else's algorithm,* someone else's vision board... and by someone else's life.

You don't even know what you really want anymore, because you've seen 100 other people's version of "success" **just before breakfast.**

Why This Is Such a Problem

Manifestation requires **emotional focus, clear desire, repetition, and depth.** Your brain is trying to lock in a pattern, but it keeps getting interrupted and distracted every five seconds.

So, you never reach complete clarity. You never embody your future. You **scroll**, compare, half-dream, and wait for the next notification, but you don't even realize it. Because everyone's doing it, it feels **normal**. And that's the dangerous part.

The brain doesn't just absorb what you want, it absorbs what surrounds you. If your environment is scattered, reactive, and noisy, your manifestation gets overwritten by **survival patterns.**

The chaos you consume becomes the code you run.

You're trying to program your future with a signal that **keeps glitching**. That's why clarity isn't optional, it's a *requirement*. To manifest anything real, your nervous system needs **safety, focus, and repetition.**

Without that, you're just daydreaming in a storm.

And the storm wins.

How to Use Tech to Power-Up Your Manifestation (Instead of Destroying It)

Here's where things get good. Tech can be your most powerful manifestation tool...**when you use it right.**

But before we dive into specific actions, let's get one thing straight: **your phone is not just a distraction machine. It's a neural gateway.**

It follows and directs your attention, it shapes your habits, and it repeats what you reward. If you feed it noise, it gives you chaos. But if you feed it intention, it becomes a tool of alignment.

Your phone is the device you interact with most in a day. **It's the greatest repetition engine in your life.** And repetition is how the brain learns. If you ignore that, you'll keep outsourcing your focus to endless scrolling. But if you learn to command it, you can turn it into **a living vision board,** an anchor, a daily ritual.

Let's start by turning your phone into a **manifestation portal.**

1. Turn Your Phone Into a Manifestation Portal

Your phone doesn't have to be a **dopamine vampire.** It can be a tool for embodied change.

Here's how:

1. Set your **lock screen** to a picture from your visualization vision board to something emotional. Not just pretty, but something that **makes you feel** intense every time.

2. Rename your **alarm labels** to say: *"Say Your Impact Rap Right Now!"* or *"Future You Needs You Today."*

3. **Record your impact rap** and set it as a **voice memo shortcut** on your home screen. Listen to it, feel it, and speak it.

4. Use a **custom notification sound** (like a heartbeat, chime, or affirmation) for when it's time to act in alignment.

These tiny changes build **repetition**, energy, and intention into your daily life. They don't interrupt; they **redirect you back into your power.**

2. Record Yourself Saying Your Impact Rap (and Listen Often)

I know we just said it, but this deserves its dedicated paragraph. **Your voice carries your vibration.** When you're in a strong state, record your Impact Rap, then say it like you mean it!

Now, play it in the background while you cook, walk, journal, drive, or move. **Let it rewire you on loop.**

You're creating an emotional anchor.

You're programming your brain passively and actively.

You're using tech to build a new identity.

That's powerful!

Every time you hear your own voice affirming your future, you're signaling your Reticular Activating System to prioritize that reality. It's not fluff, it's **neural conditioning.**

It works faster because it's personal, emotional, and rhythmic. And the more often you hear it, the more your brain starts believing it's already true. That's not just motivation. **That's transformation.**

3. Curate Your Feed Like Your Future Depends on It

Because it a way it does. If your social media makes you feel worse every time you open it, that's a sign.

Start unfollowing. Mute people. Clean up your digital environment the same way you'd clean your room before building a new life.

Follow people who make you feel **empowered, authentic, grounded,** and alive. Not just sparkly. Don't just consume. **Connect. Create. Manifest.**

And here's a radical idea: Create content as the version of you that you want to become, even if no one watches. Be the future you. Practice being visible, real, and powerful. **Be bold!** Be you!

That is high-level embodiment that will change your life!

Now you can manifest **like you mean it!**

4. Use Tech-Free Zones to Create

You don't have to throw away your phone. But you need to set some boundaries.

How about this:

- **The first 30 minutes of your day:** no phone. No scrolling. Just presence.

  Speak your Impact Rap before anyone else's voice enters your mind.

This is **prime time** for you to influence your brain.

- **The last 30 minutes of your night:** are the same. Let your RAS marinate in **your** vision, not someone else's noise.

- **One full day a week: Digital detox.** Go for a walk. Take a Synchronicity Walk like we talked about. Feel the world outside the screens. See what happens.

  When your nervous system finally gets a break, your intuition gets a chance to be heard.

A Few More Smart Tech Hacks for Manifestors

1. Make a **private music playlist** that activates your future self. Call it "My Energy Shift." Fill it with songs that pump you up, and get you going!

2. Use a **habit-tracking app** to gamify your Impact Rap practice. That way, you can achieve equal results with less effort.

3. Create a **private online photo board** for each visualization scene and look at it as often as possible when you unlock your phone.

4. Use **voice recording apps** when you're on the go, and a realization hits. Catch the fire while it's burning. The best inspirations of my life caught me in moments I didn't expect them to come.

These hacks may seem simple, but they **stack power fast.** Tech is already in your pocket! This is about turning it into a **catalyst of alignment.**

When your tools reflect your vision, every swipe becomes a command to your future.

Wait... Who's Programming Who?

You picked up your phone to change your life. And somewhere between the scroll and the search... *it started changing you.*

This chapter wasn't about hating tech. It was about realizing how quietly it can steal your focus.

How fast it can flood your brain with someone else's dreams before you even catch your own.

That ping? That post? That reel? Every one of them is a little whisper, **pulling you out of yourself.**

But you saw it now. You understood how risky that can be for your dreams. Now you can turn the whole thing around.

You stopped letting your phone be your leash and now you're turning it into your spell book. Your vision is sacred. Your time is a portal. And **your attention is the currency your future depends on.**

So here's the truth:

You don't have to quit the internet. You just have to stop letting it program you and start using it for your advantage. Now you're not just manifesting with your voice. You're doing it with your whole environment.

You are knocking this out of the park like a pro!

Final Thoughts: You're the User—Not the Used

Technology is neutral. It reflects your intention. It can enslave you or empower you. **It's your choice.** It can drain your magic or amplify it.

But only if you remember this:

Whatever you pay attention to becomes your investment. It can ruin your future or be the best decision of your life.

Choose wisely!

So the next time you reach for your phone... **ask yourself:**

Am I doing this right now to feed my dream or to hinder it?

Awareness is the bridge between your dream life and your present.

This digital age can be the most potent manifestation playground we've ever seen.

Dare to use it with purpose!

Dare to make your dreams come off the screens!

You are AWESOME!

But let me ask you something: **What are you wearing while you manifest?**

This next part might sound strange, but hear me out!

Your clothes aren't neutral. They're saying something to the world, but more importantly, to you. To your nervous system. To your identity. Every time you put them on.

You can't affirm your future self in the mirror and then **dress like you're hiding.** You can't speak power and then step into shoes that represent the version of you that **never dared to act.**

We're not talking about style here. We're talking about alignment. **Texture. Energy. Memory. Intention.**

So before we move forward pause for a second. Look at what you're wearing right now. Is it a match for who you want to become?

If not... great. Because this is where we change that.

Let's talk about clothing! Let's talk about frequency! Let's talk about **stepping into your future self, literally.**

So let's get dressed like a manifestor!

CHAPTER 8

Dress Frequency! How Clothing Rewires Your Mind To Manifest

• • •

"Put on your armor, and you will become the warrior."

— Paulo Coelho

There are doors in your reality you cannot open by thought alone. Some unlock only when your body aligns with the version of you that already has what you desire. And often, the fastest way to trigger that alignment isn't meditation, visualization, or even affirmations. Funny enough, it's clothing. You heard that right!

What you wear is an instrument of manifestation.

The science is conclusive. In a groundbreaking 2012 study published in the *Journal of Experimental Social Psychology*, researchers Hajo Adam and Adam Galinsky introduced the term "enclothed cognition."

They discovered that simply wearing a lab coat, described as a "doctor's coat," improved participants' attention and cognitive performance by over 50%. The same coat, described as the "painter's coat," produced no such effect.

Why?

Because the symbolic meaning of "doctor" triggered the wearer's brain to access sharper, more focused mental states. That's not magic. That's neurobiology.

Let me break it down: your brain assigns meaning to everything, and so it does to clothing.

A sharp blazer may represent power, a flowing dress may symbolize ease, and a hoodie might scream comfort and retreat.

When you put on your clothes, your subconscious triggers behaviors, emotions, and even physiological states that match their symbolic meaning.

In other words, you become who you dress to be.

Now, let's add another layer: your **skin**. It is your largest organ. It's not just a passive shell around your body.

It's your sensory interface with the world.

The textures, pressures, and temperatures you feel through your clothes create **neurological feedback loops** that either amplify or shut down your manifestation potential.

Research published by Field (2010) shows that certain nerve fibers in your skin, called **C-tactile** afferents, are directly linked to **emotional regulation.**

These fibers respond to soft, slow touch, the kind simulated by light, breathable fabrics like cotton or bamboo. When activated, they **lower cortisol** (the stress hormone) levels by up to **31%,** switching the nervous system from fight-or-flight mode to rest-and-digest. In this state, you become a **manifestation magnet.**

Why?

Because manifestation is not about effort. It's about aligning with your desired emotional signature; peace, joy, certainty, or worthiness.

You can't attract abundance while your nervous system is in survival mode. But you **can** when you're literally dressed in calm.

Because what you wear **isn't about how you look to others,** it's about how you feel in your own skin. It's about the inner signal you're choosing to amplify.

Every piece you put on is an invitation into a mood, a frequency. This is less about style and more about state.

What energy do you want to step into today?

What emotion do you want your body to practice holding?

You're not putting on clothes. You're putting on a feeling, a decision.

Because how you show up to your own day changes how that day shows up for you. And the energy you choose to wear helps reinforce the beliefs you aspire to embody.

So let's **get dressed with purpose,** shall we?!

Feeling anxious or stuck?

Reach for **flowy, soft clothes** in earth tones or **soft pastels.** Loose-fitting garments signal **freedom** and non-restriction to the body, countering the internal tightening of anxiety. Soft textures like cotton or modal directly stimulate your C-tactile afferents, easing your body into **relaxation.** Colors like pale blue, moss green, and light beige have been shown to **reduce reported anxiety by 39%** (Kaya & Epps, 2004).

Want to feel bold and magnetic?

Wear structured, form-fitting clothing in **power colors:** red, black, deep navy, or emerald. Choose textures with subtle resistance, like denim or firm synthetics. These activate your proprioceptive awareness (your brain's sense of your body in space), creating posture shifts and presence enhancement. The result: you carry yourself like someone **who owns the room.**

Need confidence before a job interview, date, or pitch?

Use **symbolic clothing.** Choose something associated with high-achievers, like a tailored jacket, clean white shirt, or statement shoes. It doesn't have to be expensive. The key is that you **believe** it represents competence and **charisma.**

Remember the lab coat study? That *"doctor energy"* elevated attention by over **50%?** You can create your own version of that anytime.

Don't underestimate scent and accessories. A particular perfume, bracelet, or even lipstick shade can anchor a state of mind. These are tools of **state priming.** When used consistently, your body learns, **"When I wear this, I become this."** Makes sense, right?

Let me just remind you how good that actually feels...when you're not in the mood, when everything **feels off,** and you're convinced this night is going to suck.

You're home with your girls. Someone suggests going out, and your first instinct is nope. You feel ugly, tired, maybe a little broken. Nothing about you screams fun.

But then **someone pulls out the makeup bag.** Someone else starts doing your hair. Music's playing, you start hyping each other up. Clothes start flying. Jewelry gets passed around. **An outfit you'd never dare to wear alone suddenly feels like a suit of armor.**

Two hours later you look in the mirror... and you're back. Not only looking good, but **feeling alive!** You didn't just dress up. **You are revived.**

That's not surface-level. *That's somatic.*

Touch, laughter, grooming, and presence; **this is ancient.** Your body's releasing **oxytocin, dopamine,** and probably **endorphins** too.

Your whole system gets the memo: you're safe, you're supported, and you belong.
And that belonging turns into buzz. Into joy. Into power.

Now you're not dragging yourself through the night. You're walking into it like you own it. That's the magic I'm talking about.

The clothes, the rituals, the textures, the bonding. This is manifestation at skin level.

It's not about pretending to be someone you're not.
It's about remembering who you are, together.

So don't ever underestimate the power of getting ready with the right people, the right energy, and the right intention. Because sometimes, that mirror moment is the moment everything changes.

So decide who you want to become, design how that looks like according to your beliefs, and create personas for yourself that will serve you in every way!

Like: "That's what I wear when I'm having fun. That's what I wear when **I mean business.** That's what I wear when I'm successful, when I'm happy, when I want to be magnetic, influential, convincing, or simply **unforgettable.**"

This is how you can hack your identity, one piece of clothing at a time!

If you're dressing for who you are, you stay locked in your current timeline. But if you **dress for who you are becoming,** the universe responds.

So are you ready to transform your reality while looking stylish?

Here's how to do it:

1. **Choose your desired state:** confident, relaxed, playful, abundant, sexy, spiritual, assertive.

2. **Ask:** What clothes does that version of me wear? Be specific! Colors, textures, fit, accessories.

3. **Dress in alignment** with that identity, even if it's just one piece of clothing. You don't need a wardrobe overhaul. One symbolic trigger is enough to shift your state of mind.

4. **Move, speak, and act** as if you are already that version of yourself. Clothing is the entry point. **Action** is the confirmation.

Do this daily, and you'll notice a change in your thoughts, decisions, and the opportunities you notice and attract.

This is **somatic psychology.** Through clothing, touch, and posture, you can create a fully functional system matched to your desired frequency. So don't just visualize the life you want. **Wear it today!**

When your outfit becomes an act of identity alignment, manifestation becomes less about hoping and more about *embodiment.*

As James Clear said, **"Every action you take is a vote for the type of person you wish to become."** Well, every outfit you wear is a vote too. So vote wisely! Dress with intention.

Wear the next version of you today and **watch the world bend around you.**

Scientific Sources:

1. Adam, H., & Galinsky, A. D. (2012). Enclothed cognition. Journal of Experimental Social Psychology, 48(4), 918-925.

2. Field, T. (2010). Touch for socioemotional and physical well-being: A review. Developmental Review, 30(4), 367-383.

3. Kaya, N., & Epps, H. H. (2004). Relationship between color and emotion: A study of college students. College Student Journal, 38(3), 396-405.

4. Chen, H. Y., Yang, H., Hsieh, C. L., Chen, M. C., & Chang, Y. J. (2013). The effectiveness of weighted vests on social attention for children with autism spectrum disorder. Research in Autism Spectrum Disorders, 7(1), 20-26.

Threading the Truth

There's a moment when you put something on, and your body says, "No." You feel that „no," **but you override it.** Maybe because it feels familiar. Perhaps because it's practical. **Maybe it's just what you wear when you're not sure who you are.**

But your body knows.

It remembers how you felt the last time you wore that shirt. It remembers who you were when you wore those shoes. This chapter wasn't about clothing. It was about **honesty.** About recognizing that your outfit has been echoing back an old version of you, long after **you've outgrown it.**

You started to realize that the way you dress isn't neutral. It's a rhythm. A language. A feedback loop. The next time you stand in front of your closet and pick out an outfit that aligns with who you're becoming instead of who you've been, **your body will respond.** You will carry yourself differently. Something will shift.

You don't need anyone to validate the way you show up anymore. Because, for once, **your body, voice, and intention are all facing the same direction.**

And that's how manifestation feels like when it works.

No forcing. No pretending. Just authenticity wrapped around your skin. This is how we stop treating **embodiment** like an idea and start living it as a practice.

But there's more. Something hidden in plain sight. Not an aesthetic. Not a mantra. A pattern. A formula that explains why things work out and why they don't. Why do they click one moment and collapse the very next? You've been experiencing this all along. Now It'll be revealed.

Meet F.A.T.E.

CHAPTER 9

F.A.T.E.

The Secret Formula You Were Never Meant To See

• • •

"If you don't program your own mind, someone else will."

— Unknown (attributed to many, including Napoleon Hill & Zig Ziglar)

There's something that is being used every day to control you. To sell to you. To program your behavior without you ever knowing. And it's not the Law of Attraction. It's a masterful formula that can be weaponized.

Meet **F.A.T.E. Focus, Authority, Tribe, Emotion.**

This is the blueprint used to **sell you the life you're trying to escape.** This formula isn't evil, but how it's being used in the media might be.

We're going to use it as your manifestation amplifier.

Your subconscious doesn't care whether something is true. It only cares whether it's **repeated with emotional intensity, from a trusted source, inside a tribe, and focused like a laser.**

Just think of breaking news. That's how our perceptions and beliefs are engineered, empires are built, and garbage is sold to millions. But that's also how you can **install a new identity. By hijacking your RAS to the max!**

Impressive, right? Well, I didn't invent this. The amazing **Chase Hughes,** a behavioral expert, military-level influence specialist, and one of the most dangerous minds in human behavior did. **It's time to use it for your dreams!** So, let's understand this formula one letter at a time!

F – Focus

We all know by now that our RAS filters reality based on what we focus on. It's the gatekeeper. **The pattern recognizer.** We also know that our subconscious needs narrowed, **high-contrast imagery.** Not vague wishes. If you say "abundance," it yawns. But if you say, *"I wake up at 6 am, make my morning coffee with my black Breville, check my important e-mails, and see another 3K came in,"* now, it pays attention.

It's loaded with imagery from your actual life. It's detailed, it's vivid. Now it's real!

Focus = filters. Filters = manifestations.

Your Impact Rap needs to speak about **specifics,** about the fabric of your future. You can create a new life by programming this internal „**GPS,** " which pinpoints your dreams on the map of life.

A – Authority

This one hits deep. **The brain accepts beliefs from those it sees as powerful.**

In marketing, that's a celebrity. A doctor. A uniform. A six-pack and a ring light.

What is it for you? It's the **voice you hear in your head.** If you speak your Impact Rap like you're unsure, with a shaky voice, the brain thinks it's just background noise. If you speak it like you already believe it, like a general giving orders, **the brain listens.**

Every time you show up with conviction, every time you speak like it's done, **you become your own authority.**

Authority isn't something you get. It's something you **claim.** And your subconscious listens every second to see who's in charge. Is it the old you? Or the one **who lives your dreams?**

T – Tribe

We are tribal beings. The mammalian minds don't operate in isolation. Even when you think you're making an *"independent choice,"* you're still **asking:**

"Will people like me do this?"

"Will I still belong?"

This is why most people don't change. They're not weak.

They're afraid they'll be alone.

You can manifest your vision, but if the subconscious thinks you'll be cast out from your tribe when you get it, it will quietly sabotage everything, **undercover.**

So here's a smart move:

You create a new tribe in your mind.

A new frequency of people you're stepping into alignment with. Your Impact Rap should include the social environment around you.

Like this:

"I walk with giants."

"We all speak fire and truth."

"My circle is stacked with visionaries and healers."

"We don't chase. We move."

Say it enough with conviction, and the subconscious will believe this is who you belong with.

And once it believes that?

It lets you change.

Because now you're not stepping away from the tribe.

You're stepping into a more aligned one.

E – Emotion

You know this already. If something doesn't move you emotionally, it won't move your life. It's all about intensity. Good. Angry. Grieving. Turned on. Broken. Any high emotional state becomes a **glue stick for beliefs.**

When you say your Impact Rap, it needs to feel like **a truth punch to the gut.**

Something that hits hard enough to shake your body.

Because that's how beliefs get in.

Emotion is a delivery system. A mighty one!

Without it, everything else is just theater.

The Real Revolution

This chapter isn't here to hype you up. It's here to **expose** how reality is programmed already, every single day, without you knowing. This is how advertisers, cult leaders, politicians, and master persuaders implant ideas without resistance.

But now **you've seen behind the curtain.**

Now, you have the power to stop being the target. Now, you can use this knowledge to your advantage.

To create your dream life.

*Use **F**ocus to narrow your reality.*

*Speak with **A**uthority until your brain listens.*

*Build your new **T**ribe in your lyrics and feel them.*

*Bring so much **E**motion your cells can't ignore it.*

That's Your F.A.T.E.

To start manifesting like you mean it and start installing a new self like a commander reprogramming the mind.

You've seen how they've used this model against you for decades. Now, use it for you, and watch how fast **the universe conspires in your favor.**

What Was Hidden in Plain Sight

There's a reason things haven't clicked before. Not because you didn't try. Not because you didn't want it enough. But because no one ever handed you the mechanics of how this actually works beneath the surface. This chapter cracked that open.

F.A.T.E.

Focus. Authority. Tribe. Emotion.

This **hidden mechanism,** which programs your RAS in secret, is behind every success you almost reached and every moment that felt close but fell apart.

You can't out-affirm a lack of clarity. You can't take action if your body doesn't believe it.

And you can't call something in when you're wired for avoidance.

This chapter showed you where your energy leaks and where your words get stuck. It's not about doing everything right. It's about understanding the **blueprint**.

But now you have seen the formula. Now, you have what it takes to stop guessing and start fine-tuning your RAS on purpose.

In chapter 10, we'll troubleshoot your lyrics, and excavate what is holding you back from experiencing your dream life.

Attribution:

The F.A.T.E. model, which stands for Focus, Authority, Tribe, and Emotion, is a behavioral influence framework developed by Chase Hughes, a globally recognized expert in human behavior and interrogation techniques. For more on Chase Hughes' behavioral models and teachings, visit **chasehughes.com**

CHAPTER 10

Troubleshooting & Strengthening Your Lyrics

• • •

"Doubt kills more dreams than failure ever will."

— Suzy Kassem

By now, I hope you have some badass Impact Raps in your journal. You must have spoken it, and felt its power. But what happens when you're struggling? What if doubt creeps in? What if the results aren't coming as fast as you expected? How will you handle it? How will you fix it? **How will you recognize what's wrong?**

That is where most people give up. But not you. Because **this book was built, so that you win.**

You're on the edge of a breakthrough.

And in this chapter, we will come out on the other side.

So, if you feel blocked, stuck, or that your Impact Rap isn't creating the shift you want, let's troubleshoot and refine it until it **hits big.**

Maybe your phrasing is too safe. Maybe you're avoiding the real desire. Or maybe your nervous system doesn't believe it yet.

This chapter is where we zoom in. Where we strip it down and rebuild it with truth, rhythm, and emotional voltage. **This is where your words finally land like thunder.**

1. Are You Feeling It or Just Saying It?

If your Impact Rap hasn't delivered your dreams yet, it most likely falls short because of its **lack of emotional charge.** If you say the lyrics without fully feeling them emotionally, your subconscious won't register them as truth.

Fix It:

- Stand up, move, and engage your body.

- Speak louder, with conviction. If it still feels awkward, even though you mastered your lyrics in the previous chapters, great! You're stretching your comfort zone.

- Imagine your future self saying these words after already **achieving everything you want.** Speak from **THAT** energy.

Action: Record yourself saying your Impact Rap **when you feel most confident.** Play it back when doubt creeps in. Let that confident version of you be your anchor. Every time you listen, you realign with that energy and reaffirm who you're becoming. Soon, that voice won't just be a recording; **it'll be your reality.**

2. Is Your Impact Rap Aligned With Your Truth?

As we discussed previously, when your words don't resonate deep in your gut, you'll subconsciously reject them. If something still feels off about your Impact Rap, **tweak it now!**

Ask yourself:

1. Do I actually want this, or is it what I should want?

2. Do these words feel like ME, or do they sound forced?

3. If I had to bet my life that this would come true, would I still phrase it this way?

Fix It: Adjust the language to fit your voice. If *"I am wildly successful"* feels fake, try *"I am stepping into success daily with my craft."*

Action: Rewrite any part of your Impact Rap that doesn't feel like **your absolute truth.** You must bring this home! And unless you do, it won't work. There is just no way around this one. This isn't about getting it perfect. It's about making it **undeniably yours.**

If you are struggling with this part, ask a friend to help you refine your lyrics. If that's not possible, well...technology is your ally.It's okay to get stuck. But **to** stay stuck is a choice. So don't focus on the problem, but on the solutions. Be creative, be bold, and **get out of your own way!**

3. Are You Saying It, Then Acting Against It?

If your Impact Rap says, *"I attract abundance effortlessly,"* but you constantly stress over money, while you're not doing anything to have any, **you send mixed signals to your mind.**

Fix It:

Align your actions with your words.

If your Impact Rap says you're confident, then practice small acts of confidence daily. However, that may look like. If it says you're wealthy, start managing your money with the mindset of someone with financial freedom.

Your brain watches what you do more than what you say. **When your behavior contradicts your words, the signal gets scrambled.** But when even the smallest action backs your declaration, your system starts believing it. And belief, embodied belief is what turns your Impact Rap from noise into transformation.

Action: Pick ONE action now that aligns with your Impact Rap, and do it today!

4. Are You Expecting Instant Results?

Your brain has been wired for years to believe certain things. Impact Rap is rewiring it. But just like building muscles at the gym, **it takes repetition and consistency.** Drop expectations. That's a forceful energy. It will hinder your manifestation.

If nothing seems to be happening, **ask yourself:**

1. Have I been doing this consistently for at least 30 days?

2. Am I looking for proof that it's working or proof that it's not?

3. Am I getting frustrated and blocking my progress?

Fix It:

Let go of the need for immediate results. Trust the process. **Results often come right after you are about to give up.** Right after, you let go of what should happen and when. Right after, you stop caring about it and start enjoying your impact rap.

Celebrate even the slightest shifts in mindset or external circumstances. **That's a huge achievement!**

Action: Track small wins every day. Even a tiny change in thinking is **proof it's working.** And you deserve to celebrate them!

5. Are You Speaking from a Place of Power or the Lack of It?

When you say your Impact Rap, are you speaking like someone stepping into their future or someone begging for a change without having any power?

Fix It:

1. Drop the energy of *"I hope this happens"* and step into **"This is already mine."**

2. Say it like you've already arrived. Own it. Let your tone match the power of those words.

Action: Stand in front of a mirror and say your Impact Rap as if you already have everything you're speaking into existence.

Power doesn't beg. **It declares.** And when you speak like it's already yours, you collapse the gap between who you are and who you're becoming. You're not wishing anymore. You're broadcasting truth.

And truth, when owned, bends reality.

Doesn't it feel amazing? Doesn't it feel liberating?

Sharpen the Spell

Words are power.

But sloppy words are...meh. Words you kinda-sorta mean? **They'll take you in circles for decades, it's guaranteed.** I think you probably have enough proof of that by now.

This chapter wasn't about being poetic. It was about **precision**. Because manifestation isn't about how beautiful your lyrics sound but how true they feel when you say them out loud. And if there's even a flicker of resistance when the words leave your mouth, your body feels it. Your energy stalls, and the message gets **scrambled.**

So this was the chapter where we stopped romanticizing the fluff. We got **honest** about the phrases that felt flat and the lines that sounded good but **didn't deliver**. You learned how to cut them out without feeling guilty. You learned to troubleshoot and to keep the rhythm alive.

This is the work most people skip, or they can't even bring themselves to begin.

Many people throw affirmations at the wall and wonder why nothing sticks. But you're here to craft powerful lyrics that **mean something.**

Spells that burn through the walls. The stronger your lyrics, the clearer the signal.

And when the signal is clean, the shift comes fast.

So sharpen the spell, and let's make this a lifelong fire.

In chapter 11, I'll share the ultimate shortcut between you and your future self.

Ready to step forward?

Authenticity—The Ultimate Shortcut

● ● ●

"The privilege of a lifetime is to become who you truly are."

— Carl Jung

As we discussed in Chapter 8, wearing clothes that align with our true selves is an act of authenticity. In this chapter, we will explore what it means to be authentic not only when we dress up but **in everything we do.**

So, ultimately, the **fastest way** to shorten the time between where you are and where you want to be... is to **start being authentic.**

To stop lying to the world and to yourself.

Every second you spend being someone you're not, watering down your truth, twisting yourself to be more "likable," or **pretending you don't care when you do,** is another act out of alignment with your true self. Unfortunately, it prolongs your wait.

The more you don't act like the authentic YOU, the more you'll have to wait for what you truly desire.

I'm not willing to sell you a comforting lie; I'd much rather tell you the **raw truth** because

I want you to live your dreams!

Manifestation is alignment. That's not just a cute word. It's **physics**. Frequency. **Signal and receiver.**

The real you is **magnetic**. The fake you is static and stagnant.

I don't mean the *"real you"* that was formed through wounds. I mean the real you underneath all that. The version that moves the way your soul moves.

The more you act like your authentic self, the faster your life reshapes.

Here's the truth most people can't accept:

Reality doesn't respond to what you "want." It responds to who you are (as a vibration).

When you become fully authentic, you're not only "being yourself." **You're locking yourself into the energetic signature of your most aligned timeline.** The version of you who already has the life you want.

It's not high-vibe all the time; it's not saying *"I'm grateful"* while secretly panicking. It's not pretending to be calm when burning inside. **It's real.**

That's why things show up for you faster, because your energy isn't confused anymore. The universe knows where to deliver to. **Authenticity is your correct address.**

Every time you dilute yourself, you move further away from the delivery point.

Every time you shrink, hide, people-please, or perform... you send a new signal. *And then you wonder why the dream feels so far away.*

It's not because you're not worthy. It's because the version of you who is trying to receive doesn't even match the version who ordered it. **Let me be blunt:**

Acting authentic is the ultimate manifestation technique.

And it's a bold one. A brave one. One that strips away the fluff and demands that you stop building your **self-worth** from the reactions of others.

Every day, you show up as the real you, unedited, honest, and a little messy, maybe, you „**shorten"** more and more time. **You speed up the process.** You vibrate louder. You get seen by the people meant for you. You see paths that „*didn't exist"* before. Well, you just haven't seen them.

And suddenly... what you've been trying to manifest for months shows up in days.

Why?

Because you became a match for it. Not through effort. But through truth. Through authenticity.

Now, you're probably thinking: *"But what if I don't even know who the real me is?"*

You're not alone. You've been taught to filter, shape, and perform since childhood.

You were taught who to be in order to be accepted. Not who you truly are. So yes, peeling back all those layers might take some time. But **here's the good news:**

Even trying to act just a little bit more real than the day before, moves the needle.

Every time you choose truth over performance...bam! **Alignment** happens. Every time you say what you mean instead of what sounds nice...bam! **Authenticity.** Every time you walk into a room and don't morph your vibe to match theirs...bam! **Time shrinks.**

The path between you and your dreams shortens every time you stop betraying yourself.

It's not about becoming anything. It's about remembering who you are beneath the layers of conditioning.

Let me say that again: **You don't have to become your "better self." You just have to stop hiding your true one.**

And if you're not sure what that self even looks like or feels like... that's okay. That only means it's time to go deeper. The Impact Rap method gets you moving. But unearthing your **purpose** is the single **most transformative act** you can do. It's the key that unlocks your true potential and aligns your entire life with **meaning and fulfillment.**

You have a choice to make. Keep circling the same loops, waiting for clarity to strike... Or flip the whole game and step into the life you were actually built for.

If you're ready to go deeper, into your **emotional blueprint,** your **core values**, your patterns, your power... then I've got something for you.

A system. A framework. A mirror. One that doesn't hand you generic answers. *It hands you back to yourself.*

It's called: **"The Purpose Equation—**
Find the missing pieces, shatter stagnation, and step into the life you were born to lead.

This isn't another book full of nice ideas and empty affirmations. **It's the one that ends the search.**

If you've been waiting for a green light to go full-force on becoming who you really are...this is it!

Let's collapse timelines!

Let's get **nuclear!**

Let's detonate the old story!
Let's build from truth, power, and soul!

Find **The Purpose Equation** on **Amazon.**
And **start living like your life actually matters.**

Nothing Sticks Without the Real You

You can have all the words. You can have the rhythm. You can even have the perfect vision. But if it's not true, if you're still hiding a layer of yourself to stay likable, polished, polite...**it won't hold.** Not in your mind, not in your life, not in the world.

This chapter wasn't about impressing others but about **expressing your true self**. Exposing the parts of you you were hiding out of fear all along.

Your dream life doesn't respond to the mask. It responds to what's raw, honest, and slightly terrifying to say out loud. It responds to the real you. You saw how easy it is to build a Rap that sounds powerful...but isn't entirely yours. How easy it is to aim for success, but subconsciously according to someone else's definition. And you saw what happens **the moment you drop the act.**

The Rap hits harder. The vision sharpens. The **resistance fades,** not because you pushed through it, but because you finally stopped pretending.

Authenticity isn't a vulnerability trick. It's a frequency that **cuts through the noise faster than anything else**, because manifestation always accelerates when you act in alignment with your truth. The real truth.

Final Thoughts: No More Filters

From here on out, it only works if you're honest. No more borrowed dreams. No more polished lines. No more filters. **No more pretending.**

Saying no, if you mean no, and yes only if you genuinely mean it.

Let your voice reflect your actual self, your deepest truth, not your projections. Say it how it wants to be said. Even if it's messy. Because when you're fully you, **you won't need permission slips anymore.**

But I don't want this only to be a short-lived flicker for you. **I want your flame to burn and outlast all storms!**

Not just for a day, not just for a week.

I want you to **lock it in for life!**

So, **let's make it last.**

CHAPTER 12

Lock It In For Life

• • •

"We are what we repeatedly do. Excellence, then, is not an act, but a habit."

— Aristotle

In this chapter, we will build systems that hold you accountable when you want to quit. **We're going to develop habits that can outlast your bad days.**

But first, I want to speak to the ones who gave up somewhere in this process but picked this book off the shelf once again with one last ounce of hope in their hearts.

You are a trooper!

If that's not you, *congratulations*! Skip ahead to the next page.

But if it's you, let me give you a *virtual hug*.

You didn't fail; you are just tired. And you are not the only one.

> *If you only knew how many times I almost gave up the things dearest to me.*

Maybe you got discouraged, but it's **NEVER too late to step into your power.** Let me help you find your way again, so you get to experience **how amazing it feels to be your authentic self fearlessly.**

Now, I want to address those of you who *made it here with a bang!* **You guys knocked it out of the park!**

You are the proof that it works!

You hold the torch of hope for everyone else to see that it's possible.

Thank you from the bottom of my heart because you're not only helping yourself but helping everyone else reading these lines.

Whether you've been consistent or let life get in the way, **we will fortify your habits, forge your dreams into reality,** and make this so effortless, so automatic that you never *"fall off"* track.

I want all of you to **win**! I want you to live with no regrets.

So let's lock it in for life!

Let's explore how to make Impact Rap something you never *"forget."* Let's make it part of who you are.

This isn't a task. It's supposed to be **fun!** Not like doing laundry or washing the dishes.

Let's go back to the beginning.

1. Reignite Your Why – And What's at Stake If You Stop?

Why did you start in the first place? What were you hoping would change? What future were you creating?

Now, imagine never following through. Imagine waking up a year from now, ten years from now, and realizing **nothing has changed besides you getting older**. The same struggles, doubts, and cycles run your life because **you let your vision slip away.**

Now, flip the script! Imagine if you had stayed consistent. Imagine how much clearer, stronger, and more aligned you'd be.

Imagine the happiness, freedom, joy, and connections you would have in that reality.

That version of you is right here!

But you have to show up.

Open up your journal, and start immersing yourself in the **lyrics of your dreams again.**

Action: Say it out loud, say it proud! Your impact rap is your anthem.

2. Make It Fun, Not a Duty

If Impact Rap ever felt like something you *"had"* to do, don't worry. We will change that! It's time to shake things up.

Here are 5 ways to make it fun:

1. **Turn It Into a Game** – Set a challenge: How fast can you get into peak energy while saying your Impact Rap?

2. **Use Music** – Find an instrumental beat that excites you and say your Impact Rap over it.

3. **Do It with a Friend** – Find someone to practice with and hype each other up!

4. **Mirror Work** – Say it while looking into your eyes, like speaking to your future self.

5. **Make It Dramatic** – Shout it. Whisper it. Say it like you're in a movie scene. Play with it!

Action: Pick ONE of these methods and do it right now. Feel the difference it makes. Or **try all of them!**

Alternate them every day!

Make it fun, make it an adventure!

3. Create Triggers That Make Impact Rap Automatic

Your brain loves habits. We know all about it.

So when you tie your Impact Rap to something you already do, it becomes effortless.

Easy Ways to Make It a Habit:

1. Say it every morning before brushing your teeth.

2. Say it before you start work.

3. Say it before a workout.

4. Say it right before bed.

5. Set it as a phone reminder that pops up daily.

6. Write it on sticky notes and stick them everywhere in the house so you can see them daily.

Action: Choose one habit trigger right now and commit to it. **Alternate them or do all of them every day.**

4. Let It Evolve With You

Your Impact Rap isn't meant to be static. As you grow, it should grow, too.

If it ever starts feeling stale, that's a sign you've outgrown it.

Signs It's Time to Upgrade Your Impact Rap:

- It doesn't excite you like it used to.

- You've already achieved part of what you were manifesting.

- You feel like a new version of yourself, and your old words no longer fit.

Action: If your Impact Rap feels outdated, **tweak it!** Add stronger words. Make it sharper, bolder, more YOU.

Or make entirely new ones!

So let's summarise how you can lock it in for life!

Built to Stay

This was the chapter where everything shifted from *"practice"* to *"pattern."* Where Impact Rap stopped being something you do and started becoming something you are.

You've seen what's possible when you **speak with conviction.** When you move with clarity. When you get honest about what you want, what you believe, and **what you're done apologizing for.**

But none of them lasts if you don't commit to making them habits.

You saw how the brain rewires when you show up consistently. You felt how something small, like repeating lines with rhymes or adjusting a phrase, can ripple through your day and **propel you forward.** You realized that mastery isn't about doing more.

It's about doing the righ thing until it becomes part of your life, your instinct, your habit.

This is how you lock it in. This is how the shift holds.

So here's what you do now. **Print it. Speak it. Listen to it on a loop.** Move when you say it. Adjust it when it dulls. Do it like **your life depends on it,** because **in a way** it does.

The Power of Repetition —Your 30-Day Challange

As we know, your brain loves patterns. It learns through repetition, forming **neural pathways** that reinforce behaviors and beliefs. The more you repeat something with emotional intensity, the faster it becomes your reality. Now, we're going to use it in a **30-day challenge!**

Commit to 30 days of daily Impact Rap practice.

1. Speak your Impact Rap every morning and every night. Say it like **you're not asking anymore.** Say it like you're already there. Then, prove it with one small action.

2. Track your emotions before and after saying your impact rap, and **notice any shifts.**

3. Journal about the experience. **Every little detail could potentially change your life,** so don't miss any.

4. Adjust your lyrics as you see fit, especially if the noise creeps in. Let your Impact Rap **evolve with you.**

5. Make sure you **keep it fun.** You want to stay in the manifestation energy, remember? *Not in a forceful one.*

Stepping Into Your Power

You now have a tool that most people will likely never discover.

A way to rewire your mind, activate your vision, and step fully into the life you were meant for, fueled by habit and emotions.

The question is: **will you use it?**

Will you stop after day 30 or even before that? Or will you **keep going until you live your dreams?**

This is **your moment of triumph!** No more waiting. No more hoping. You know what to do.

The Manifestation Revolution is yours.

Everything you once hoped for is **now unfolding before your eyes.** This isn't a dream anymore. **You made it real!** I couldn't be more proud of you all!

You are on a journey worth taking, one that worth every step! One that brings real transformation and fulfillment.

Can't wait to hear your **success stories!**

Manifest Like You Mean It –
Your Questions Answered

Q1: Do I really need to believe in this to make it work?

You don't need blind faith. You need momentum.

When you start doing, even a little, the synchronicities and shifts begin. Belief builds **after** movement, not before. So no, you don't need to "fully believe." You just need to **start**.

✦

Q2: I've tried affirmations before. How is Impact Rap different?

Impact Rap asks you to **say it like you mean it.** To move with it, to feel it. You bring your body alive. Your voice now is a powerful outlet. Your energy can radiate. That creates belief. Impact rap involves rhythm, rhyme, and emotions. That's radical!

Q3: What if I feel fake doing it?

You're not faking the dream; you're stretching into it. It's unfamiliar territory. Refine the words and lines, then add rhythm so your body stops resisting it and starts vibrating with it.

$$\bigstar$$

Q4: Can I use music with Impact Rap?

Sure, if it helps. But **you don't need it.** You are the beat. You are the rhythm. Some days, it'll feel like poetry. Others, like a war cry. Go with what moves you. You can do whatever feels good as long as it works for you.

$$\bigstar$$

Q5: How long does it take to see results?

Sometimes minutes. Sometimes months. The more emotionally honest, aligned, and consistent you are, the faster the world starts echoing back. But it's not about time. It's about **your signal strength.**

Q6: What if I don't feel anything when I do it?

Then you're probably holding back. Loosen your body, your shoulders. Stand tall. Breathe deep. Say your impact rap with conviction until something in you shifts. **Meditate** if you need to, or take a walk.

Maybe you aren't really aligned with the lyrics. Perhaps you need to ask those deep questions again. Go back to the earlier pages in the book and figure out what moves the needle for you. What is truly important for you? Then, create lyrics in alignment with that. Asking a friend to help you craft your impact rap can be a fun idea!

✦

Q7: Do I need to do it daily?

Not rigidly. But consistently. **Repetition trains the subconscious.** Think of it like brushing your brain clean every day, removing the dust of doubt. I would advise you to do it every other day at least, but if you want to go all in, then do it 3 times a day, every day! Why not? We want results, right? Then let's get it!

Q8: Can I do it silently in my head?

You can. But spoken word + movement has more voltage. Your body is the amplifier. Whispers don't always change the world. **Declaration does.** Impact rap was meant to be said out loud, like you mean it!

✦

Q9: What if I laugh or feel weird doing it?

Good. That means you're expanding. Laugh, enjoy that moment! Shake it off, then do it again, louder. Magic doesn't live in your comfort zone. If it feels funny, so be it! Own it!

✦

Q10: How do I know what to rap about?

Start with the version of you you're becoming. What does he believe? How does he act? What does he feel? What does he create daily? And why? Figure out who you want to be, and start writing the life or your future self. That's your script.

Q11: Can I do this if I'm going through a hard time?

Especially then. Your voice is a powerful transmutation tool. Write your heart out! Spill your pain into ink. Let that experience be the very tool to heal.

✦

Q12: Do I have to visualize while doing it?

You don't have to close your eyes. But see it. Feel the room shift. Act like you've stepped into it. Your body knows the way before your mind does. Your impact rap was designed to be combined with a visualization that matches the scene to your lyrics.

✦

Q13: What's the science behind this again?

It's rhythm. Repetition. Emotion. It taps into your Reticular Activating System **(RAS)**, which filters what you notice. Speak with intensity, and your brain re-calibrates what it believes to be "real."

Q14: Is this manifestation or something else?

It's manifestation but with the brakes off. It's not the fluff, and it's not passive. Not polite. Not pretty. It's full-body, full-volume, fire-lit co-creation with the universe.

✦

Q15: What if I'm scared to want what I want?

Then Impact Rap is your safe space to practice wanting out loud. Say it scared. Say it trembling. But say it anyway. The fear won't last. But the results will. Don't let the shadows stop you from living your dreams.

✦

Q16: Do I have to follow the exact format in the book?

No. It's the opposite. I want you to write your own.

This isn't doctrine. It's creation. I want you to have your own voice and win! Tell the world who you are out loud!

Q17: Can I do this with others?

Yes. And it's a powerful idea. Syncing up with aligned people creates energetic force fields. Impact rap together! Rhythm is contagious. So go and make some waves out there!

✦

Q18: What if it's not working for me?

Then, check your signal. Are you speaking from your head or from your gut? Are you repeating words or living them? Are you rushing or resonating? Adjust. Drop expectations. They are forceful energy. What you need is a relaxed manifestation state. Do whatever makes you feel that way.

✦

Q19: What if I'm afraid I'll manifest the wrong thing?

You can't manifest what's not aligned with your energy. The more you speak what you think you want, the faster you'll feel if it's false. Trust that feedback. Then, adjust the lyrics to be a more authentic one. Don't be afraid, be conscious.

Q20: How often should I update my Impact Rap?

Every time you evolve. Every time you outgrow the words. When it feels too small, too stale, or not electric enough, it's time. Impact Rap is alive. Let it breathe with you. It's a practice that can enhance your life, just like meditation.

✦

Q21: What if I don't feel "worthy" of what I'm trying to manifest?

The first thing to do is remove resistance. I suggest you do shadow work to find out what is causing such friction. Try using the questions in chapter 6 to get to the root of it.

✦

Q22: Is this spiritual? Or psychological?

It's both, as far as we know it. It's spiritual, and it's neuroscience. It's about energy, emotion, and creation. Synchronicities. Experiencing something we might deem extraordinary. What is it? You decide.

Q23: Do I need to know how to rap?

Not at all. I'm not a rapper myself by any means. This isn't music. It's you expressing yourself but with rhythm. You don't rhyme for style; you rhyme for subconscious impact. You're not performing for an audience. You're speaking to **yourself**.

Q24: Can I do this in a whisper if I can't be loud?

Absolutely. Your mind will hear you. What matters is that you mean it! What matters is that the lyrics are true. So don't worry about the small things; focus on your impact.

Q25: What if I cry during Impact Rap?

Then you're doing it right. It should move you, one way or another. If it doesn't, then something is wrong. Tears are emotions leaving your system. Let them flow. They're tension-releasing. Let them flow. You are healing, and the lyrics are the medicine.

Q26: Is this for healing or success?

Well...what do you need it for? It is what you make it to be. Impact Rap rewires the filter that affects **everything**: self-worth, action, and pattern recognition. Use it to heal if you need to heal. Let it be your aid. Use it to create success, if that's your deepest desire, but here, I wonder: What is success about for you? What do you truly want? Why? Maybe go back to chapter 6 and, once again, clarify.

✦

Q27: Can I use this for relationships?

Yes. Speak love into your reality. Rap about aligned connection, emotional safety, and mutual passion. But remember: you're not trying to control others. You're aligning with what's true for you. And let me tell you from experience, sometimes what you manifest becomes your lesson. Manifest wisely.

Q28: What if my dream changes?

Let it be. Dreams are not contracts. They're invitations. Update your Impact Rap as your clarity sharpens. What matters is that you stay **100% authentic,** whether it's about your dreams or about your lyrics. Keep it real!

✦

Q29: Will this make me passive? Just talking instead of doing?

Not a chance. Impact Rap is **action.** It's mental rehearsal, emotional priming, and full identity embodiment. And from that energy, your real-world action becomes unstoppable. **This is 100% action.**

✦

Q30: What if I forget to do it for a few days or weeks?

Let's be honest. You didn't forget it. It was no longer your priority. Reignite why you started the first place. This will put you right back on track! You can absolutely nail this! Let's go!

Q31: Can I teach this to my kids or clients?

BIG Yes! I feel honored. Lead by example. Let them see how you speak powerfully. Let them feel how dreams aren't something you think, but *something you make happen.*

Q32: Why does this work better than just visualizing quietly?

Visualization is the scene in your mind. Impact Rap is the supercharger that can influence your RAS and render your dreams into your actual reality. I'm not saying visualization alone can't do that, but why wouldn't you want to make your manifestation 10x more powerful?

Q33: Should I do this before bed or in the morning?

Whenever you need to **charge your system.** Morning sets the tone. Evening rewires your rest. Make it a habit! Do it as often as you possibly can. Do you wish to have results? Well, then, you need to put in the work. Luckily, this is fun!

Q34: What if nothing happens right away?

Drop all expectations because they can hinder your manifestation. Focus on your why rather than your immediate results. Keep going. You're doing great!

Q35: Can I use this method to overcome fear?

Yes. Fear is energy without direction. Impact Rap gives it rhythm, form, and a powerful release. It can anchor you back into power. It's not just manifestation. It can be used for **regulation too.**

Q36: How do I keep this from becoming just another to-do list item?

Don't make it a chore. Say it during fun activities. Make impact rap exciting and liberating. If you feel like it's becoming a chore, impact rap is not the problem. You probably just need to have more fun without fixating on impact rap.

Q37: What if I'm manifesting something "big," like a life overhaul?

Then, your Impact Rap becomes your **daily recalibration.** Big dreams require a strong signal. The greater the shift you wish to create, the deeper your embodiment must be. Say it like you mean it. Say it until your life bends.

✦

Q38: How do I know I'm doing it "right"?

You will feel something. You will feel different like something is happening. You are **activated.** Your words will land heavier. Your body says: "Message received; I'm working on it. "

✦

Q39: Can I use this to break bad habits?

Yes, because it shifts identity. You don't just stop doing something. You **become** someone who doesn't need it anymore. Use Impact Rap to speak as **that** version of you. Watch your habits catch up.

Q40: What if people think I'm crazy doing this?

Let them. You're not here to be understood by everyone. You're here to align with your dreams. You are not trying to impress the world. I'm all about expressing your authenticity. People will judge. But now, you are stepping into power.

Share your Experience
Your Story Could Change Someone's Life

You know what it's like to search for answers, crave a breakthrough, and wonder if something will ever work. Now imagine someone else, right where you were, hovering over this book, unsure if they should leap.

Your experience could be the reason why they say yes to themselves and to their dreams.

If this book sparked something in you and made you feel empowered to take action, **share that.**

Your words could be exactly what someone else needs to see before they step into their transformation.

What spoke to you the most?

What would you say to someone who's considering reading these lines?

What shifted in you?

Take a moment to **leave a review on Amazon.**

Your story has an **IMPACT.**

Let it be the light someone else needs.

Join the Impact Rap Movement – Share Your Video!

Now that you have your powerhouse Impact Rap, let's take it to the next level!

Be part of the Impact Rap movement! It's time to show the world how powerful you are!

Here's how you can get involved:

Record yourself performing your Impact Rap—it doesn't have to be perfect, just real. Don't make another perfect-looking social post; **just be you** and perform your Impact Rap in a way that feels good!

Upload it to Instagram with the hashtag #MyImpactRap

Tag me (@start.with.purpose) so I can share the best ones! Be authentic!

Challenge a friend to make their own Impact Rap and share their video to keep the movement going!

Let's make this go viral!

Imagine thousands of people Impact-Rapping their dreams into reality.

It starts with YOU. TODAY!

Ready to Go Even Deeper?
Go Deeper. Get Clear. Act Now.

RADICAL CLARITY BREAKTHROUGH EXPERIENCE
2×2-Hour Private Sessions
Real-time. No-fluff. Purpose discovery through deep, guided activation.

Some breakthroughs need more than journaling or waiting for clarity to arrive on its own.
You **can** find your purpose alone — but why stay stuck in fog when you could walk straight through it with a guide?

Imagine being truly seen.
Imagine finally naming the thing you've felt for years but couldn't explain.
Imagine walking away with a direction that clicks — in your **gut**, not just your mind. **This is that moment.** You can **finally connect the dots!**

What We'll Do Together:

1. Uncover Your Inner Framework
Reveal inner conflicts and unmet needs
Identify your core values — what *actually* matters to you
Pinpoint your true purpose — beyond ego, roles, or survival

2. Align With What's Already Inside You
Discover your innate strengths — the gifts you've underused
Surface real passions — not hype, but the deep, fire-in-the-belly kind

3. Break the Freeze
What's really held you back?
Why haven't you done it yet?
We remove the emotional friction so clarity flows — fast.

4. Design the ACTION PLAN
Build your purpose-driven roadmap
Lock in the truth:
→ Action crushes doubt, hesitation, and overthinking
→ Action becomes proof — and proof builds momentum

5. Your Dream-Life Blueprint
Clarify aligned, authentic goals
Anchor a vision that pulls you forward — and build the plan to reach it.

This is not inspiration. This is transformation.

"I was stuck in loops — overthinking, doubting, pretending I didn't care. This experience shattered that. I left with a deep sense of direction, like I'd finally met the real me. I wish I'd done it years ago."
— *Leila M., Germany*

You'll walk away with:

✔ Deep clarity on who you are
✔ A blueprint for real momentum
✔ Tools to rewire old resistance
✔ A direction that makes sense — and feels like *you*

Spots are extremely limited.

Once they're gone, they're gone.

Scan the QR code below and never live another day without doing what you truly care about!

What's next?

Your journey doesn't end here. The adventure continues with **The Purpose Equation,** the book that will help you uncover your core values, deepest passions, and unique strengths. It's a step-by-step guide to uncover your **Purpose Ecosystem,** the internal structure that fuels the life you were born to lead.

You'll gain the missing puzzle pieces. The building blocks you've been searching for. And once you put them together, you'll **unlock a lifetime of unstoppable momentum.**

Now that you know how to manifest like a master...

It's time to live your purpose boldly.

Your next chapter starts now.

Find it on **Amazon,** or always at startwithpurpose.online

This Is Where You Pass the Torch

You've made it. You read this book for a reason. But maybe it wasn't only for you. If this book ignited even the slightest flame in you, imagine what it could do for someone else stuck in the dark. **I'm asking you to be part of a treasure hunt!**

So here's your next move if you are holding the paperback: Leave this book somewhere unexpected. **On a train seat. At a coffee shop**. In a waiting room. Or at an airport, maybe on a seat while you wait for your flight. **Somewhere, someone could find it when they need it most.** *Let it live beyond you. Let it travel the world. Let it find its next owner.*

Reading the e-book or listening to the audiobook?

Consider grabbing a paperback, and becoming part of the ripple. There is magic in passing it forward, hand to hand. Because maybe this isn't just a book. Maybe it's a spark that can ignite the entire world.

And you're now a part of it.

Post a photo of where you left the book using **#ManifestItForward**, and tag me: **@start.with.purpose**

If You Happened to Find This Book

... left on a bench, in a café, on a bus seat, then something rare just happened. *You stumbled into a quiet revolution.* You've been handed a spark, not by chance, but by someone who believes in something bigger than themselves: **you.**

This book is part of a movement, **a living pulse of purpose passed hand to hand, heart to heart.**

So now, you're a part of it, too.

If this book lit something in you, don't let the spark die here. **Pass this copy forward** and let it find the next soul just like it reached you.

Or keep it as your own torch to revisit, underline, and return to when the fire fades. Then buy another copy to **kick off a new chain.**

Leave it somewhere.

Write a message and light the world again!

This isn't just a book. It's a movement. And now **you can be the reason** someone gets lit up!

Keep the magic alive!

Available in paperback and e-book format.
Audiobook coming soon!

Thank You

Thank you for your time. One of the most valuable things in the universe.

Thank you for your presence and for your **unwavering heart,** which kept beating forward even when things felt uncertain. You still dared to look behind the curtain. You kept going. That matters more than you know.

Thank you for sharing this earth with all of us. Your existence is not an accident.

Your journey is significant.

We are all here with a **purpose,** for a reason. And yours is unfolding right now.

So, thank you for your bravery, your commitment, your light.

You are part of something much **much bigger.**

Let's keep lighting the path for each other.

If You Are Still Here, Amazing...

Because I have something to share:

The Moment That Changed Everything

It wasn't planned. But it split me open. It hit like lightning.

I was just running a simple errand—a totally normal day. And in minutes, everything changed. Not in theory. Not in mindset. **My soul was shaken awake.** It had nothing to do with vision boards. Nothing to do with journaling. **I found Purpose.**

Not as a concept, but as a living, breathing force. And once I saw it, I couldn't unsee it.

I can't explain it all here. But if you've ever felt like something vital is just beneath the surface or wondered why you're really here—then **my next book is a must read!**

The Purpose Equation.

What happened that day unlocked everything for me. It become **the best day of my life.**

And I can't wait for purpose to change everything for you, too.

Messenger Page

Whether you bought this book, or found it by chance, leave one sentence for the next soul who opens it.

What was the most powerful insight it sparked in you?

What wisdom do you want to pass forward?

Tell them where you found this book , or where you're leaving it next. **Be the messenger.**

Keep the magic going.

✦

Messenger Page

Messenger Page

Messenger Page

Messenger Page

Messenger Page

Messenger Page

Messenger Page

One Last Spark

If one of these handwritten messages stopped you, moved you, or cracked something open—**capture it.**

Take a photo of the page that hit the deepest.

Let the ripple echo beyond this book.

Tag me on Instagram: **@start.with.purpose**

Your share could reach the next soul who needs it most. This isn't just a story passed on

It's a signal lit.

You're part of the pulse now.

Keep the magic pumping.

I'll see you in the next one!

Bianka

Printed in Dunstable, United Kingdom